JOHN UPDIKE

MODERN LITERATURE MONOGRAPHS

GENERAL EDITOR: Philip Winsor

In the same series:

S. Y. AGNON   *Harold Fisch*
SHERWOOD ANDERSON   *Welford Dunaway Taylor*
LEONID ANDREYEV   *Josephine M. Newcombe*
ISAAC BABEL   *R. W. Hallett*
SIMONE DE BEAUVOIR   *Robert Cottrell*
SAUL BELLOW   *Brigitte Scheer-Schäzler*
BERTOLT BRECHT   *Willy Haas*
JORGE LUIS BORGES   *George R. McMurray*
ALBERT CAMUS   *Carol Petersen*
WILLA CATHER   *Dorothy Tuck McFarland*
JOHN CHEEVER   *Samuel T. Coale*
COLETTE   *Robert Cottrell*
JOSEPH CONRAD   *Martin Tucker*
JULIO CORTÁZAR   *Evelyn Picon Garfield*
JOHN DOS PASSOS   *George J. Becker*
THEODORE DREISER   *James Lundquist*
FRIEDRICH DÜRRENMATT   *Armin Arnold*
T. S. ELIOT   *Joachim Seyppel*
WILLIAM FAULKNER   *Joachim Seyppel*
F. SCOTT FITZGERALD   *Rose Adrienne Gallo*
FORD MADOX FORD   *Sondra J. Stang*
JOHN FOWLES   *Barry N. Olshen*
MAX FRISCH   *Carol Petersen*
ROBERT FROST   *Elaine Barry*
GABRIEL GARCÍA MÁRQUEZ   *George R. McMurray*
MAKSIM GORKI   *Gerhard Habermann*
GÜNTER GRASS   *Kurt Lothar Tank*
ROBERT GRAVES   *Katherine Snipes*
PETER HANDKE   *Nicholas Hern*
LILLIAN HELLMAN   *Doris V. Falk*
ERNEST HEMINGWAY   *Samuel Shaw*
HERMANN HESSE   *Franz Baumer*
CHESTER HIMES   *James Lundquist*
HUGO VON HOFMANNSTHAL   *Lowell W. Bangerter*
UWE JOHNSON   *Mark Boulby*
JAMES JOYCE   *Armin Arnold*
FRANZ KAFKA   *Franz Baumer*
RING LARDNER   *Elizabeth Evans*
D. H. LAWRENCE   *George J. Becker*
SINCLAIR LEWIS   *James Lundquist*
GEORG LUKÁCS   *Ehrhard Bahr and Ruth Goldschmidt Kunzer*
NORMAN MAILER   *Philip H. Bufithis*
BERNARD MALAMUD   *Sheldon J. Hershinow*
    (*continued on page 150*)

JOHN UPDIKE

Suzanne Henning Uphaus

FREDERICK UNGAR PUBLISHING CO.
NEW YORK

Copyright © 1980 by Frederick Ungar Publishing Co., Inc.
Printed in the United States of America
Design by Anita Duncan

Library of Congress Cataloging in Publication Data

Uphaus, Suzanne Henning, 1942–
    John Updike.

    (Modern literature monographs)
    Bibliography: p.
    Includes index.
    1. Updike, John—Criticism and interpretation.
PS3571.P4Z93   813'.54   79–48076
ISBN 0–8044–2934–0
ISBN 0–8044–6945–8 (pbk.)

For Bob
who makes it all possible

Contents

Chronology

1932	Born in Shillington, Pennsylvania, only child of Wesley and Linda Grace Hoyer Updike.
1936–50	Attends Shillington public schools.
1945	Moves with family to a farm outside of Shillington.
1950	Enters Harvard University on full scholarship.
1953	Marries Mary Pennington.
1954	Graduates summa cum laude from Harvard. Sells first story to *The New Yorker*.
1954–55	Attends the Ruskin School of Drawing and Fine Arts in Oxford, England, on a fellowship.
1955	Daughter Elizabeth born. Moves to New York City.
1955–57	Employed as "Talk of the Town" reporter for *The New Yorker*.
1957	Son David born. Resigns from *The New Yorker* and moves to Ipswich, Massachusetts.
1958	Publishes *The Carpentered Hen* (poems) and *The Poorhouse Fair* (novel).
1959	Son Michael born. Publishes *The Same Door* (short stories).
1960	Daughter Miranda born. Publishes *Rabbit, Run* (novel).
1962	Publishes *Pigeon Feathers and Other Stories*.
1963	Publishes *The Centaur* (novel) and *Telephone Poles and Other Poems*.
1964	Receives National Book Award for *The Centaur*. Publishes *Olinger Stories, A Selection*.

1964–65	Travels to Russia, Rumania, Bulgaria, and Czecho-slovakia as part of the U.S.–U.S.S.R. Cultural Exchange Program.
1965	Publishes *Of the Farm* (novel) and *Assorted Prose*.
1966	Receives O. Henry Award for "The Bulgarian Poetess." Publishes *The Music School* (short stories).
1968	Publishes *Couples* (novel).
1969	Publishes *Midpoint and Other Poems*.
1970	Publishes *Bech: A Book*.
1971	Publishes *Rabbit Redux*.
1972	Publishes *Museums and Women and Other Stories*.
1973	Travels on State Department tour to sub-Saharan Africa.
1974	Separates from wife and moves to Boston. Publishes *Buchanan Dying*, a play.
1975	Publishes *A Month of Sundays* (novel) and *Picked-Up Pieces* (prose).
1976	Divorces. Publishes *Marry Me*, a novel.
1977	Marries Martha Bernhard. Publishes *Tossing and Turning* (poems).
1978	Publishes *The Coup* (novel).
1979	Publishes *Too Far To Go* and *Problems* (both short stories).

Introduction

Perhaps no contemporary author can match the overwhelming variety of Updike's publications. There is Updike the generous and amiable critic; Updike the urbane short-story writer for *The New Yorker;* Updike the playwright, wresting a historical figure from anonymity; Updike the poet, too obviously struggling with words and rhythms; and most important, there is Updike the novelist, for whom words and rhythms often achieve a breathtaking lyricism.

When we talk of Updike the novelist, we are again astounded by his range. There is the sympathetic treatment of a dying generation in *The Poorhouse Fair,* the explicit sexuality and ambivalent protagonist of the Rabbit novels, the mythical comprehensiveness of *The Centaur,* the comedy of *Bech,* the pastoral world of *Of the Farm,* the sensational suburban decadence of *Couples,* the sermons of *A Month of Sundays,* the domestic turmoil of *Marry Me,* and most recently, the Islamic marxism of *The Coup.*

But in the midst of this diversity there are certain elements common to all of Updike's writing. Most important, there is Updike's remarkable mastery of language. For example, Updike's descriptive power is based on a skillful use of particular detail and an unerring sense of rhythm. He often uses these talents to recapture a mood from the past, evoking in the reader a sense of wistful nostalgia. In this example of sustained lyric in-

tensity, Rabbit is in the smoke-filled dimness of a bar,
listening, as a black woman named Babe plays the piano:

What does Babe play? All the good old ones. All show
tunes. . . . "My Funny Valentine," "Smoke Gets in Your
Eyes," "I Can't Get Started," starting to hum along with
herself now, lyrics born in some distant smoke, decades
when Americans moved within the American dream, laughing at it, starving on it, but living it, humming it, the
national anthem everywhere. Wise guys and hicks, straw
boaters and bib overalls, fast bucks, broken hearts, pent-
houses in the sky, shacks by the railroad tracks, ups and
downs, rich and poor, trolley cars, and the latest news by
radio. Rabbit had come in on the end of it, as the world
shrank like an apple going bad and America was no longer
the wisest hick town within a boat ride of Europe, and
Broadway forgot the tune, but here it all still was, in the
music Babe played, the little stairways she climbed and
came tap-dancing down, twinkling in black, and there is
no other music, not really. . . .

Often Updike seems to be stretching the possibilities
of the written word as far as they can go. Sometimes
the experimentation will take the form of steadily ac-
celerating, extraordinarily long sentences, in which detail
is piled on detail, leading the reader, breathless, to a
delightfully comic denouement. Among my favorites are
these sentences, in which the African protagonist of *The
Coup* remembers his undergraduate days at McCarthy
College in Franchise, Wisconsin:

This prairie's harvest celebration came at McCarthy each
November, in the Thanksgiving football game against our
arch-rival, Pusey Baptist, an even more northerly academic
village of virgins and bruisers that, for the four years of my
undergraduate career, was four times narrowly defeated—
in 1954 by an intercepted pass, in 1955 by a goal-line stand,
in 1956 by a heroic, dodging, arhythmical, incredible end
run by a sandy-haired instant legend who next year died
uncomplainingly of leukemia, and in 1957, most thrillingly

for us non-gringos, by a field goal kicked sideways, soccer style, from the forty-three-yard line by a Peruvian general's degenerate son, who had gone out for the team as a way of making homosexual contacts.

Equally entertaining is his description of the postfootball libations:

I licked my lips, remembering the beer in the frats afterward, where the Pusey Baptists were invited to drown their annual sorrow, and the rugs stank like swamps of hops, and the exceptional co-ed, liberated without a restraining philosophy of liberation, liquidly consigned herself, in a ratty upstairs chamber, with hip-hoisted skirt and discarded underpants, to a line-up of groggy, beefy ejaculators.

Updike's mastery of diction is most apparent in the variety and authenticity of his characters' voices. There is the minister:

"To those who find no faith within themselves, I say no seed is so dry it does not hold the code of life within it, and that except a corn of wheat fall into the ground and die, it abideth alone; but if it die, it bringeth forth much fruit. Blessed, blessed are the poor in spirit."

The black militant:

"Hell, man, there was *heat*, right? I thought lynching time had come, I didn't know there wasn't twelve hundred crackers out there, I was in no shape to take care of some whitey woman, let Whitey take care of his own."

The jealous mother-in-law:

"Everything wakes me now," she said. "Even your bed seemed noisy to me last night."

The quarreling siblings:

"Joanna thinks she's a big shot because she has a boyfriend."

"I do *not*. Mommy, he's always saying I have a boyfriend when I don't. He's always telling lies. *Liar*. Big shot. Liar."

The rhetoric of the American politician as he does a little hustling:

"Our technical boys can mop up any mess technology creates. All you need here is a little developmental input, some dams in the wadis and some extensive replanting with the high-energy pampas grass the guys in the green revolution have come up with. You have a beautiful country here, basically, and we're prepared to make a sizeable commitment to its future."

And the young child, trying to understand:

"Daddy?"
"What?"
"Is baby Becky dead?"
"Yes."
"Was she frightened?"
"Oh no. No. She wasn't frightened."
"Is she happy?"
"Yeah, she's very happy now."
"Good."
"Don't you worry about it."
"O.K."
"You snuggle up."
"Yop."
"Think about throwing stones."
"When I grow up, I'll throw them very *far*."
"That's right. You can throw them pretty far now."
"I know it."
"O.K. Go to sleep."

But behind a conversation such as this, there is something deeper than a rare verbal talent. Updike's greatest gift is the profound sympathy for his characters that his narrative voice conveys. Updike has said that an author "must only love" [1] his fictional characters, and in many passages of the novels this love becomes a deep understanding and compassion, creating powerful moments of emotional intensity. Perhaps the most painfully moving is the scene in *Rabbit, Run* in which Janice, disoriented by drink, accidentally drowns her infant daughter in the bath:

With a sob of protest she grapples for the child but the water pushes up at her hands, her bathrobe tends to float, and the slippery thing squirms in the sudden opacity. She has a hold, feels a heartbeat on her thumb, and then loses it. . . .

She lifts the living thing into the air and hugs it against her sopping chest. Water pours off them onto the bathroom tiles. The little weightless body flops against her neck. . . . A contorted memory of how they give artificial respiration pumps Janice's cold wet arms in frantic rhythmic hugs; under her clenched lids great scarlet prayers arise, word-less . . . for all of her pouring prayers she doesn't feel the faintest tremor of an answer in the darkness against her . . . and she knows, knows, while knocks sound at the door, that the worst thing that has ever happened to any woman in the world has happened to her.

This is the responsive, the *human* artist, combining his verbal talent with an understanding and compassion for his characters that few novelists achieve.

Perhaps this compassion for the human condition arises from Updike's own experience of intense despair; he has said, "I've touched a kind of bottom, when I've felt that existence itself was an affront to be forgiven." [2] The common theme behind Updike's writing is the pro-found religious searching that grows from this despair, a quest in which doubt fights desperately with faith. "Without the supernatural," Updike has said, "the nat-ural is a pit of horror." [3]

These two worlds, the natural and the supernatural, are present explicitly or implied in all of Updike's work, and they are basic to an understanding of it. In his writ-ing there is always the physical, natural world, apprehended by the body through its senses and appetites. But there is also another, supernatural world (whether Christian, classical, or Islamic), apprehended by the soul, through faith.

Thus Updike sees man as a dichotomous creature, split between his physical desires on the one hand and his spiritual yearnings on the other. In Updike's fiction the protagonist's spirit cries out for expression. But because faith is so difficult in a contemporary world that is indifferent to spiritual values, the protagonist often loses his vision and devotes himself to the natural rather than the supernatural, the carnal rather than the spiritual. At moments of epiphany he may temporarily be transported by his body's physical action, to a sense of religious meaning. But these moments are rare and transient, and more often the Updike protagonist, in his desperate search for significance, finds that his spirit is suffocated by the material world. For in all the novels except *A Month of Sundays* the natural and the supernatural, the physical and the spiritual dimensions of man, stay stubbornly apart. They fail to integrate.

According to Updike, sex is the closest to a religious experience that the physical world provides, so the protagonist often searches for spiritual satisfaction in sexual encounters. He seeks the ideal lover who will provide for him the transcendent experience. But Updike is always aware that sex is, finally, a natural rather than a supernatural experience. The protagonist's search for spiritual satisfaction becomes futile and promiscuous, often resulting in his recognition of this futility and his acceptance of one sexual partner. Such an acceptance signifies the resignation of the protagonist's spirit.

While this acceptance of one woman, one job, and family responsibilities may seem ethically admirable to many, Updike is always suspicious of ethical action, believing that it hides an impoverished spirit. Thus his novels are often peopled by altruistic Christians who substitute ethical, social, action for religious faith. While these characters might be heroes for other writers, Updike consistently undermines their stature in his own novels. Updike's novels suggest that involvement in ethical action is a barrier to faith rather than a means to its fulfillment. From this we can understand Updike's uneasiness with the theology of Paul Tillich, because of its emphasis on Christian action in this world.[4] Similarly, we can understand his attraction to the theologian Karl Barth, who described God as "Wholly Other," and whom Updike has described as an "anti-humanist" theologian.[5]

Updike would never agree that "God is dead." Our very search for Him implies His presence. But we live at a time when there is little faith and much doubt. Updike has said, "I've felt in myself and those around me a failure of nerve—a sense of doubt at the worth of any actions. At these times one has nothing but the ancient assertions of Christianity to give one the will to act."[6] Updike, more than any other contemporary American author, traces again and again the difficulty, almost the impossibility, of maintaining these "ancient assertions of Christianity" today. At the same time he repeatedly asserts the desperate need, the intense and irrepressible hope for religious faith.

Perhaps this profound absorption with religion is a result of being raised in a family that, Updike has said, used to "examine everything for God's fingerprints."[7] Born in 1932 to Lutheran parents of Dutch and German ancestry, Updike was raised in Shillington, Pennsylvania, by both parents and grandparents. The family was poor, supported only by his father's teaching at Shillington High School. But they were also well educated, and they focused their hopes on their only child, who showed an early aptitude in art. When they moved to a farm outside of Shillington, Updike was increasingly isolated from his own age group; in this atmosphere he concentrated his attention on his drawing and writing talents.

Updike's mother was particularly ambitious for her son. Having noted that Harvard had produced more than its fair share of authors, she became determined that John should go to Harvard. She had a strong interest in writing, taking correspondence courses and later publishing some of her own stories. After an aunt gave eleven-year-old John a subscription to *The New Yorker*, he decided that his goal in life was to publish in that magazine, probably as a cartoonist.

Updike won his scholarship to Harvard; his family could hardly have afforded to send him there otherwise. There, he published a number of cartoons, poems, and essays in *The Lampoon*. This, combined with the social contacts, produced a public self-confidence and ease that have developed into a generous social amiability over the years. As an undergraduate he met and married Mary Pennington, a Radcliffe fine-arts major.

After his marriage and graduation, Updike went to Oxford, England, on a fellowship to study art for a year. During this year he published four stories and ten poems in *The New Yorker* and was offered a job as their "Talk of the Town" reporter. The couple moved to New York City for a few years. Then, with a growing family, Updike resigned his job with *The New Yorker* and moved to Ipswich, Massachusetts, to become a novelist. His first novel was published in 1958, and within twenty years he had published twenty more books, nine of them novels.

Updike lived in Ipswich from 1957 until 1974, becoming involved in Ipswich activities as a member of the Congregational church, the local Democratic committee, the golf club, and an amateur musical group. In 1974 Updike separated from his wife and moved to Boston. Following his divorce, he married Martha Bernhard in 1977. The Updikes now live in Georgetown, Massachusetts, a few miles from Ipswich.

Because of the sheer volume of Updike's work I will

be unable to discuss the minor publications in this study but will concentrate on the novels, with a final chapter on the most popular short stories. I will refer to the other works only as they relate to these more major ones. After all, it is as a novelist that Updike is most widely recognized, and it is in writing fiction that his greatest talent lies.

1

The Poorhouse Fair

When *The Poorhouse Fair* appeared in 1958, reviewers announced the arrival of a rare new talent to the American literary scene. Indeed, *The Poorhouse Fair* is a remarkable achievement for a first novel. Written by a young man of twenty-six, it sympathetically portrays people three times that age. The character of Hook, we know from Updike himself, is based on his memories of his grandfather, who lived with Updike's family when the author was growing up. Similarly, the poorhouse is based on Updike's memory of a poorhouse in his home town. But these memories are transformed into a novel that is profuse with imagery and dense with symbolic detail.

The events of *The Poorhouse Fair* span a single day at a rest home for old people in the not-too-distant future. It is the day set aside each year for the old people's fair, when they sell their handicrafts to the public. By dividing the novel into three parts, each recounting events of the morning, the afternoon, and the evening of that single day, Updike has reinforced the sense that a way of life is ending as the novel concludes with the old people going to sleep in the darkness.

At the beginning of the novel the old people are setting up booths for the fair on the poorhouse grounds, stringing colored lights and setting out their handicrafts. The director, Conner, has predicted a clear day, even as clouds gather in the skies above. We meet Conner, first in his office in a cupola of the poorhouse, high above the old folk, and then as he descends and wanders among their displays, suggesting rearrangements. Too old and frail even for a booth, Hook also wanders among the tables. He particularly admires a patchwork quilt that becomes symbolic for him, with each design evoking a cherished memory or belief.[1]

Gregg, years younger than Hook but still a resident of the old folks' home, is also wandering the grounds. He sees an old and crippled cat and brings it into the grounds hoping to cause trouble; his purpose is always to be disruptive of any established authority. When Conner sees the cat he orders his assistant, Buddy, to shoot it. While Buddy follows orders, the truck with soft drinks for the fair arrives, and under Gregg's directions the driver backs into the poorhouse wall, crumbling it. As the first drops of rain begin to fall, the old people are summoned to lunch, and the first section ends.

Part 2 opens with lunchtime conversations. As Conner enters the dining room many of the old people remember their former director, Mendelssohn, with fondness. Mendelssohn, now dead, would begin lunch with hymns outside under fair skies; instead, Conner has brought them inside to eat without singing. After lunch Conner goes to the lounge where Hook and other old people are talking. At first they do not notice him, so Conner starts a fire in the fireplace, using copies of a religious magazine, hoping his presence will be revealed by "a triumphant burst of flame." But the fire only smokes, the flue is closed, and one of the old people has to help him by opening it.

Meanwhile Gregg and a few other old men have gotten a bottle of liquor, forbidden to them, and are gathered around a "common cup," getting increasingly drunk. As they drink, the rain lifts, and the old people excitedly prepare their booths for the fair once more.

As part 3 opens, Conner, concerned that the rubble

of the broken wall will reflect on his management of the home, directs the old people in clearing it up. As he tosses the pebbles into the wheelbarrow, Gregg deliberately flips one too far; ignored, he stones Conner again. Stirred by the momentary fear in Conner's face and their cumulative resentment of him, several old people join the attack. Hook, who has been studying the sky, belatedly sees what is happening. Just as Conner turns on the old people, saying "I know you all," they retreat, and only Hook is left behind. Conner mistakenly assumes Hook was the instigator of the incident and angrily forbids the shaken old man to smoke the cigars that are his only physical comfort.

The fair begins, and most of the remainder of the novel describes the people who crowd into the poorhouse grounds. They are "a race of pleasure seekers," and their gossiping involves holidays, illicit affairs, physical ailments and their cure. The only exception is one old man here with his grandson, whose conversation with Hook laments the decline of the old values.

Conner, in his office, attempts to explain the stoning as motivated by the old people's jealous recognition that "he was better than they." He is only concerned that the public not hear of it. When Buddy puts his arm around Conner, the director draws back. Rebuffed, Buddy joins the crowd at the fair, telling about the stoning, ridiculing Conner. As night falls the old people retire, and the novel ends focusing on Hook, awake and troubled in his bed, asking himself whether there is some way he can establish contact with Conner.

Updike's dualism is nowhere more obvious than in this first novel. The characterization of Conner and Hook simplifies what is, according to Updike, man's basic duality, by the division of the body and the spirit into two separate individuals, devoted, accordingly, to the natural and the supernatural worlds. There is Conner, the atheistic, ambitious manager of an old people's home, who concerns himself exclusively with the physical comfort and health care of his wards and is unable to understand that the aged inmates are spiritually unfulfilled. Then there is Hook, aged and dying inhabitant of the rest home, who has the spiritual vision and the religious insight that Conner lacks. The novel revolves around these opposing viewpoints, but it clearly shows American society as moving toward Conner's philosophy, becoming obsessed with the body, its health, its sexuality, and its comfort, believing that man is nothing more than a physical animal.

Conner is dedicated to this world because he believes there is no other. He devotes himself in a seemingly selfless manner to the alleviation of bodily suffering, for he believes that the body is all man is. "We've sifted the body in a dozen directions, looking for a soul," he tells Hook. "Instead we've found what? A dog's bones, an ape's glands, a few quarts of sea water, a rat's nervous system, and a mind that is actually a set of electrical circuits." The previous manager of the home let its physical environment deteriorate to what were, for Conner, shocking standards of neglect. Conner has, consistent with his philosophy, improved the residents' food, their health record, and the appearance and comfort of the poorhouse. He has put in windows and fire escapes. But Conner's changes have conveyed to the inmates a denial of any life after the death that they are, in spite of all Conner's improvements, so close to.

Conner's work as manager of the old people's home is, he believes, part of the great humanitarian drive toward the creation of a utopia of physical satisfaction and comfort. When asked by the old people how he envisages heaven, Conner describes a heaven on earth:

"There will be no disease. There will be no oppression, political or economic, because the administration of power will be in the hands of those who have no hunger for power, but who are, rather, dedicated to the cause of all humanity. There will be ample leisure for recreation. . . . The life span of the human being will be increased to that of the animals, that is, ten times the period of growth to maturity. . . . There will be no poor. . . . No pain and above all no *waste*. And this heaven *will* come to *this* earth, and come soon."

The credibility of Conner's viewpoint is consistently undercut by Updike's criticism of his ignorance of human nature, including his own. What Conner believes is his altruism, Updike exposes as self-love. Conner likes to think of himself as unselfish and dedicated, with "no hunger for power," yet he imagines himself talking about his improvements at the poorhouse to "grateful delegates" who listen "admiringly." Near the end of the novel he ponders the possibility of promotion by the state: "Wherever I can serve, he told himself. At the same time his mind ran off a film. He was sitting at a table of dignitaries, not in the center but with becoming modesty at one end. He rose, papers in hand. 'My department is pleased to report the possession of evidence which would indicate,' he said, and paused, 'that the cure for cancer has been found.'"

Far more ominous than this self-deception is Conner's failure to recognize the animal streak of malicious and instinctive cruelty in human nature. He fails to discern Gregg's undisciplined and destructive rejection of all authority. While Hook recognizes Gregg as a malevolent child who must be controlled, Conner consistently misinterprets Gregg's character, thus giving Gregg the opportunity to create the chaos he craves. Gregg is responsible for the incident with the cat, the breaking of the wall, and the stoning of Conner. Similarly, Conner never realizes that Buddy will maliciously ridicule him when his homosexual advances are rejected.

Updike emphasizes that Conner himself has the same malicious potential. When Conner orders the killing of the cat, which in its frailty, its imperfect eyesight, and its vulnerability reminds us of the old people, he hears the gunshot with pleasure, thinking of the progress effective "once his old people were gone." Although Conner's first response to the stoning is patterned on Christ-like forgiveness, the novel ends ominously with him trying to settle on a more suitable punishment.

Updike uses the same events and characters of the novel to criticize Conner and his purpose and to give Hook's spiritual insights unquestionable validity. For instance, Hook predicts rain while Conner fails to see the gathering clouds. Moreover, Hook recognizes that Conner and all others who seem to work for the general good are actually acting out of self-interest. Hook knows the potential destructiveness inherent in human nature; he warns Gregg not to antagonize Conner, and he remembers the cruelty and torture that even children are capable of.

Hook's faith is not in man and scientific progress, but in God and his divine purpose. His faith is based on "inner spokesmen," God-given, innate from birth, moving us toward virtue. These spiritual voices are as real for Hook as physical facts; we are born with them "as we are born with ten fingers."

These inner spokesmen respond reciprocally to the natural world of creation. For Hook, the visible universe is "an unfailing source of consolation." Hook sees a flower's creation as proof of God, Conner sees it as an accident of inevitable evolution. In nature Conner sees mostly nothing; he tells the old people, "The chief characteristic of the universe is, I would say, emptiness," but Hook finds even his little fingernail a miracle of creation. Just as Hook looks at a patchwork quilt on display at the fair and sees each design as symbolic, so does he look upon each object in the natural world as carrying symbolic meaning.

Updike has used the overriding metaphor of sight

to emphasize the opposing beliefs of Hook and Conner.
Conner has perfect sight, but he is spiritually blind;
Hook's eyesight is weak, but he has spiritual insight,
perceiving a significance to the natural world that Conner
is blind to. Conner's keen eyesight divides and differen-
tiates by paying attention to detail. Like a scientist, he
categorizes and ultimately dehumanizes on the basis of
his observations. As he describes to several old people
the heaven on earth that he is working toward, Conner
wonders if one of the old women could be classified
"technically," as "a dwarf. He wondered what the technical definition of a dwarf was."

In contrast, Hook's spiritual vision is combined with
failing physical sight. He is unable to see close-up detail;
he is described, appropriately, as "far-sighted." His
religious faith is matched in the novel by that of one
other old person, Elizabeth Heinemann, who has been
blind since childhood. She says the objects of this world
"lead me truly" toward salvation, and the biblical ca-
dences of her speech contrast with the predominantly
empirical language of Conner.

Updike's use of the metaphor of sight reveals his
suspicion that the body and the senses are barriers to
spiritual fulfillment. Elizabeth Heinemann reminds the
old people that we are taught to close our eyes to pray.
Because Hook and Elizabeth cannot see clearly, their
spirits flower, unencumbered by the physical data most of
us focus on.

With the younger people in the novel, Updike shows
us the inevitable result of an exclusive focus on man
rather than God. The people younger than Conner concentrate their eyesight entirely on the body until it becomes their religion. The teenage driver of the soft drink
truck has a girl friend who belongs to a secret club called
the Nuns, whose members let men see, but not touch,
their bodies. She has undressed before him "and lay
there on the back seat of the car while he kneeled be-

side her, his hands folded in obedience at his chest," as if in worship. In the closing description of the fair, young girls parade, naked, before the headlights of a car full of teenage boys. "We promise on a stack of telephone directories that nobody'll touch you," the boys tell them. (It is a sign of the times that telephone directories have replaced Bibles).

When this life is all there is, the priests of the new body worship become the medical scientists who prolong physical life. Thus the doctor at the poorhouse is appropriately named Angelo, his nurse is Grace. One of the counterpointing conversations at the fair concerns the illness of a child whose eyes have swollen shut. Telling her doubting husband to "have a little faith" in the doctor, the girl's mother takes her to a physician, a priest who restores physical, not spiritual, vision.

In this first novel Updike shows us that the increasing domination of the physical world in our lives, our focus on the satisfaction of the body, its comfort, health, sensual pleasure, and longevity, all these have shifted our attention from those spiritual ideals with which religion is concerned. Throughout the novel we are made aware of the spiritual superiority of the American past by dense imagery. For example, the careful craftsmanship of earlier American carpenters, most obviously displayed in the mansion that is now the poorhouse, has been replaced, wherever possible, by metal and synthetic materials. For Hook, carpentry is a holy profession because Christ was a carpenter, and he often uses wood and woodwork as analogies for spiritual values.

Just as technology has replaced wood with metal, so has it replaced the natural fire of wood and lightning with the fire of atomic bombs. Conner imagines he can control fire by installing fire escapes, but his lack of control is revealed when he makes a fire that produces only smoke. Hook knows that fire is God's natural force, which he will use to cleanse and renew.

Supported by this imagery, the two main characters and their philosophies attempt to dominate the poorhouse, image of America itself. Conner's and Hook's visions are mutually exclusive. For the former to succeed, the latter, more spiritual way of life must die, as Hook, and all the old people, soon, inevitably, will.

The Poorhouse Fair is like a tapestry dense with images; it is highly artistic in a consciously contrived, almost stylized manner. The lyricism and metaphorical resonance of Updike's language are occasionally breathtaking. Yet the form of the novel is more a series of tableaux than a plot with character development and compelling action. The characters are one-dimensional, lacking the problematical tension between the body and spirit that Updike's later protagonists incorporate. Updike has said that all his novels have an equivocal "yes, but" quality,[2] but in this first novel the "yes" is louder, the qualifications far fainter, than in any other. We must turn to Updike's second novel, *Rabbit, Run,* for thematic complexity, depth of character, and emotive power.

2

Rabbit, Run

Rabbit, Run has elicited a spectrum of responses so varied
that it is difficult to believe that critics are writing about
the same novel. Many first reviewers admired Updike's
style but repudiated the novel, emotionally offended. Re-
cent criticism often identifies *Rabbit, Run* as the most
powerful of Updike's novels. Yet its ability to offend
remains. Many of my students find *Rabbit, Run* the most
disturbing novel they have read. I would argue that these
reactions prove the artistic success of the novel, for it
is Updike's deliberate purpose to discomfort his readers,
evoking ambiguous and even contradictory responses to
his characters and imagery. Updike intentionally leads
his readers to an uncomfortable ambivalence that mirrors Rabbit's own experience. Faced with irreconcilable
conflicts, our first response may be, like Rabbit's, to run.

    Rabbit, Run is divided into three sections that move
inexorably toward the death of the baby and the irresolution of the conclusion. When it opens, Harry Angstrom,
twenty-six-year-old former high-school basketball star
nicknamed Rabbit, is on his way home from work as a
kitchen gadget demonstrator. Remembering his days of
high school glory, Rabbit joins a kid's basketball game,
then runs the rest of the way home. There he finds his
pregnant wife, Janice, mindlessly watching TV and drinking in their squalid, cramped apartment. She requests
that he pick up their son, get their car, and buy her a

pack of cigarettes. Leaving the apartment, Rabbit feels
trapped by petty demands. When he goes to pick up his
two-year-old son, Nelson, Rabbit sees him through a window, happy with his grandparents. Rabbit leaves him
there, gets the car, and drives away almost impulsively,
determined never to see his hometown again.

Rabbit heads south, but then, driving west to avoid
Washington and Baltimore, he turns onto secondary and
even more minor roads. He becomes hopelessly lost,
circling aimlessly through the long night, checking maps,
asking for directions. Finally he turns north, instinctively
finding his way back to his hometown, where he puts
himself in the care of his high school basketball coach,
Marty Tothero.

Later that day Tothero, an old man trying to recapture his youth, arranges for his much younger girl
friend to bring an extra girl, Ruth, for a dinner four-
some. After dinner Rabbit goes to Ruth's apartment,
where they make love. He decides to move in with her,
but returns to his apartment to get his clothes. As he
expected, Janice has gone to her parents' and the apartment is empty, but Rabbit is spotted by Janice's parents'
clergyman, Jack Eccles. After Eccles unsuccessfully attempts to persuade Rabbit to return to Janice, he makes
an appointment with Rabbit to play golf the following
week. The first section ends with this golf game, and
with Rabbit's elation as he hits the perfect golf shot.

Section 2 begins with Rabbit working at a job that
Eccles got for him as a gardener, responding fully to the
natural world which he is bringing to bloom. We learn
that Ruth is pregnant with Rabbit's child, but that she,
silently resenting his irresponsibility and lack of perception, has not told Rabbit. When they meet a former
boyfriend of Ruth's, Rabbit is overcome with jealousy
and hatred of her promiscuous past. He asks her to do
everything for him sexually that she had done for her

boyfriends, including fellatio, an act that she finds hu-
miliating, and that he associates with total wrongdoing.

That same night Eccles calls Rabbit to tell him Janice
is in the hospital having the baby. Rabbit leaves Ruth.
With the birth of their daughter, he becomes reunited
with Janice. He sleeps fitfully, bothered by thoughts of
death, as he waits with Nelson for Janice's return from
the hospital. He begins work with Janice's father as a
used-car salesman. When Janice does return, Rabbit is
disturbed and aroused by her milky maternal sensuality.
With Eccles's encouragement, Rabbit goes to church, but
at the service he is only aroused by Eccles's wife, an
attractive, flirtatious tease whose seeming offer he turns
down in deference to Janice. That evening, he tries to
make love to Janice and she rejects him. He leaves, wandering through town all that night and the following
day, looking for Ruth, looking for a way out of the
trap he feels he is in.

Janice, terribly upset over being abandoned again,
particularly afraid of her mother's condemnation, drinks
heavily all night and the next day. Attempting to give
the baby a bath in preparation for a visit from her
mother, Janice, disoriented by drink, lets the baby drown
in the tub.

Section 3 opens with the consequences of this death.
Returning to Janice, Rabbit turns the horror of the baby's
death over and over in his mind, feeling guilt for his
part in it. But at the burial Rabbit becomes convinced
that the baby has ascended to heaven. He feels elated,
so moved by the service and his religious certainty that
Janice's expression, "dumb with grief, blocks the light."
He tells her, "Don't look at *me*. . . . I didn't kill her."
As he tries to explain that he understands that she is a
victim too, that it's all right because the baby has reached
heaven, he sees rejection and incomprehension in the
faces all around him, including Janice's. He runs from

the cemetery into the surrounding woods and up the mountain. But, distraught, he returns to the city and Ruth. Revealing her pregnancy to Rabbit, Ruth delivers an ultimatum to him—divorce Janice and marry her. But as the novel ends Rabbit is running from Ruth, feeling trapped by her demands as well.

Many critics have identified Rabbit's running as a religious quest, a search for meaning beyond the natural world.[1] Unlike all other characters in the novel, Rabbit senses the supernatural and searches for it, convinced that "somewhere behind all this . . . there's something that wants me to find it." But Rabbit cannot find that "something" in a contemporary society that is spiritually suffocating. Thus, in *Rabbit, Run,* Updike conveys the confusion, meaninglessness, and uncertainty in American society today. Nor does Updike come to us as one who pretends to know the answers to Rabbit's, and our, dilemma. Instead there is a profound uncertainty, what I would call an intellectual honesty, in the searching exploration of this theme.

Updike conveys this complexity, this absence of absolutes and answers in our society today, by evoking in the reader ambiguous responses to the characters and images of the novel. Thus the reader is pulled one way and then another, feeling conflicting responses that make the experience of reading the novel similar to Rabbit's own experience within it.

First, our mixed admiration and condemnation of Rabbit, our ambivalent responses to him, create feelings of unresolved ambiguity. Certainly our first response is to condemn Rabbit's repeated flight, his retreat from difficulties he cannot solve. Our traditional conception of heroic action does not involve running away. The consequences of Rabbit's continuous flight tend to be destructive rather than constructive.

Yet we admire Rabbit's spiritual drive, his unwillingness to compromise. He resists the squalid, the servile,

and the commonplace, the corroding hypocrisy of a love-
less marriage, the fraud of being a gadget demonstrator
or a used-car salesman. Rabbit believes that "somewhere
there was something better for him than listening to
babies cry and cheating people in used-car lots."

At one point Rabbit explains to Eccles: "I once
played a game real well. I really did. And after you're
first rate at something, no matter what, it kind of takes
the kick out of being second rate. And that little thing
Janice and I had going, boy, it was really second rate."
When Eccles exhorts him to accept his responsibilities as
a family man, and "be mature," Rabbit identifies maturity as "the same as being dead." And indeed, maturity,
settling "into the nationwide rhythm" of meaningless
and monotonous work, devotion to family, the acquisi-
tion of material objects, *may* imply spiritual death.

The closest Rabbit can come to the "something better" he is searching for is in a sensual experience. But
for Updike the body can never satisfy the needs of the
spirit. In tying himself down to physical experiences in
which he seeks religious meaning, like basketball, or
golf, or sex, Rabbit ties himself down to a contemporary
physical world that prevents spiritual faith while it demonstrates the need for it. Yet the hunger for a transcendent belief is what prevents Rabbit from accepting
the quiet desperation of the majority. While he is unwilling to accept the second rate, he is unable, through
the course of the novel, to find anything meaningful,
permanent, and first rate.

Each of the sports Rabbit adopts is analogous to
sex, and all sex is analogous to religion in Rabbit's mind.
Rabbit's youthful basketball prowess is inextricably linked
with the sexual in his mind: "There was you and sometimes the ball and then the hole, the high perfect hole
with its pretty skirt of net. It was you, just you and that
fringed ring, and sometimes it came down right to your
lips it seemed." When Rabbit made love to his high-school

sweetheart "the two kinds of triumph" (basketball and sex) "were united in his mind."

The game of golf, like basketball, is also analogous to sex, and in his first golf match with Eccles, Rabbit is initially infuriated by his impotence. He associates the irons with Janice; when the iron refuses to hole the ball, he uses a heavier wood, which he associates with Ruth. With them both, "home is the hole." Finally, the successful swing with which the first section of the book ends, unites religious, sexual, and sports diction to demonstrate a temporary union of these elements in Rabbit's life. The ball he hits defies the physical laws of gravity and achieves a kind of immortality: "his ball is hung way out," and "Rabbit thinks it will die" but it does not. When Rabbit triumphantly cries "That's *it!*" he is describing a unity of purpose and action that eludes him in real life.

But Rabbit comes closest to a religious experience in the ceremonies and rituals he attaches to sex. His initial sexual advances to Ruth involve cleansing, kneeling, and talk of their "wedding night." But sex is not enough; at the moment of sexual release he feels despair. Part of the sexual ceremony with Ruth involves pulling down the bedroom shade, an act which, significantly, blocks out the stained-glass window of the church across from her apartment.

Our admiration for Rabbit's stubborn search for meaning in a world that is no longer spiritually meaningful clashes with our disapproval of his habitual flight, thus creating our ambivalent response. The reader is not alone in his mixed admiration and condemnation of Rabbit. Ruth loves him because he hasn't "given up," because, she says, "in your stupid way you're still fighting." Yet she hates his irresponsibility. Similarly, Eccles works hard to return Rabbit to his family, yet he admires and even envies Rabbit's spiritual hunger, his sense of the supernatural. The minister wants "to be told about

it, wants to be told that it is there, that he's not lying
to all those people every Sunday." Moreover, both Ruth
and Eccles are astonished and envious when, in separa-
rate conversations, Rabbit professes his belief in God.

Rabbit runs . . . yet we are sympathetic—what is a
mere human, or as one critic puts it, a "non-hero" [2] to
do? What religious experiences has contemporary society to offer? Attachment to the mother, the wife, the
lover, the coach, one's lost youth, none of these is a
satisfying substitute for the meaningful religion of the
past. It is because society no longer offers the satisfaction of a traditional religion that Rabbit must hopelessly
search for meaning elsewhere. And when all else fails,
the ambiguity of the contemporary human condition is
reinforced. The final lesson is perhaps one of compromise with the world as it is.

In the final moment of the novel Rabbit looks at
the church window outside of Ruth's apartment, representative of the hope he once had for religious meaning:

Afraid, really afraid, he remembers what once consoled
him by seeming to make a hole where he looked through
into underlying brightness, and lifts his eyes to the church
window. It is, because of church poverty or the late summer
nights or just carelessness, unlit, a dark circle in a stone
facade. There is light, though, in the streetlights.

So has contemporary American society substituted secular
for religious light.

The intentional ambiguity that Updike has created
in our response to Rabbit is reinforced by our similarly
mixed response to Eccles. While Rabbit's actions are far
from heroic, Eccles *does* try to act by the traditional
standards of heroism, that is, helping others and sacrificing himself in the attempt. Throughout the novel Eccles
doggedly persists in his attempts to track Rabbit down
and reunite him with his family. While we may initially
admire this seeming unselfishness, Updike gradually reveals Eccles's motivation as selfish.

The return of Rabbit to his family becomes for
Eccles a test of his own values, which put social responsibility above spiritual fulfillment. If Rabbit rededicates
himself to his family, Eccles's belief in ethical standards
of behavior will be verified.

But Updike knows what Eccles suspects, that ethical
action in this world is not enough. Christianity is not
external actions, mere adherence to ethical standards.
These are a poor substitute for a spiritual commitment
that transcends this world. Thus Updike briefly introduces
us to another minister, Kruppenbach, contrasting Eccles's
belief in ethical action with the fervent faith of a near
mystic.

Eccles goes to Kruppenbach to "talk over" the problem of returning Rabbit to his family, but Kruppenbach,
the Angstroms' Lutheran pastor, will have none of it. He
says "all this decency and busyness is nothing," that the
role of the minister is not to be a "cop" or an unpaid
therapist. Instead, a clergyman should be "an exemplar
of faith," so much so that the strength of his conviction
will overcome the parishioners' fear of death and assure
them of an afterlife. A clergyman's duty is to focus on
the supernatural, not the natural world. "There is nothing
but Christ for us," Kruppenbach tells Eccles. But Eccles
lacks Kruppenbach's spiritual certainty and must fill the
void with the "busyness," the "meddling," that Kruppenbach deplores.

Updike takes care to evoke a negative response to
Eccles. For instance, in several passages he emphasizes
Eccles's inherent adolescence. Like Rabbit's former basketball coach, Tothero, Eccles craves the company of
younger people and spends a great deal of time gossiping
with teenagers at drug store soda counters "so he comes
home titillated silly with 'how far' you can 'go' on dates
and still love Jesus. . . . He loves kids; their belief is
so real to them and sits so light."

Our mixed response to Eccles is also colored by our

gradual recognition that his emphasis on ethical responsibility is destructive rather than redemptive. Eccles's
wife traces the chain of responsibility for the baby's
death to her husband, saying, "You never should have
brought them back together. The girl had adjusted and
something like this never would have happened." Eccles
agrees that the death is indeed his fault, but even after
the drowning he continues his efforts to keep Janice and
Rabbit together. He believes "marriage is a sacrament."
But there is irony in this conviction too, for Eccles spends
his time patching up the marriages of others, while his
own marriage is disintegrating from lack of attention.

In making all these points Updike is generating disapproval in the reader's responses to Eccles; at the same
time he includes details in Eccles's characterization that
prevent simple disapproval and cause us to sympathize
with him. For example, we learn that Eccles chose the
ministry as a futile attempt to win the approval of his
stern and forbidding father. Eccles's response to children is just the opposite to sternness. Although we are
amused by the way his daughter manipulates him, we
respond to him warmly in the consistent understanding
and concern that he shows Nelson, the child whom almost everyone else has forgotten.

But the most important factor that makes our response to Eccles partially sympathetic is his self-knowledge, his recognition that he is as lost as Rabbit is. He
is locked into the natural world with no perception of the
supernatural, preaching the gospel of moral action and
hiding his spiritual inadequacy from others to save his
sense of worth. Eccles recognizes his own lack of faith
and feels despair. After he hears of the baby's death
he tells his wife, "I don't believe in anything." But still
he must continue the role that society has accorded him,
breaking tragic news, comforting the bereaved, conduct-
ing funeral services. The events of the novel age Eccles
visibly, as his wife perceives with resentment. Indeed,

her nagging, pseudo-psychological criticisms of Eccles
also evoke our sympathy for him.

Updike's careful characterization of both Rabbit and
Eccles creates the reader's ambiguous response to the
novel. On the one hand, the whole foundation of social
stability which Eccles stands for, church, family, responsibility, and commitment, is threatened by Rabbit's irre-
sponsible actions. On the other hand, we admire Rabbit,
who, unlike Eccles, refuses to compromise, refuses to be a
hypocrite and accept half-truths, until, at the end of the
novel, he realizes there are no whole truths to be had.
It is this absence of absolutes in contemporary society
that the novel portrays, and this ambiguity is reflected
in Updike's imagery as well as his characters.

Updike uses religious images in *Rabbit, Run* to demonstrate the confusion and contradiction that Rabbit experiences. He does this by, first, evoking the traditional
religious associations of the images, their former function as a connection with the supernatural. This done,
he just as deliberately strips them of their religious
connotations, to show that these meanings are no longer
applicable for Rabbit or the reader. As we read, at first
we attach a fixed religious expectation to each of these
images that they ultimately do not fulfill. Thus we are
caught in an ambiguous situation which mirrors Rabbit's
own. Having come to expect these meanings, as Rabbit
expects the light to be on in the church window, we
experience Rabbit's own frustration when Updike col-
lapses the images' traditional connotations.

For example, when the second section of the novel
opens with the scene in the garden, Updike carefully
builds up our traditional associations of gardens as nature
divinely sanctioned. In Western thought gardens have
been, from the Garden of Eden, symbols of the correspondences for which we yearn. At first these correspondences are evoked by Updike's religious word
choice: this garden has "trumpets," "warm ashes," and

"God Himself." It reminds visitors of heaven. It is Horace's garden, reminding us of the poet Horace who found solace in his garden. But Horace Smith, called Harry for short, is dead, and the garden he planted is being tended by his flirtatious widow and another Harry, a rabbit whose function in the garden is appetitive.

The garden, however, does not lead Rabbit to spiritual analogies; it is not evidence of divine harmony for Rabbit. Instead, the correspondences which Rabbit makes are entirely physical, from natural object to natural object, flowers to women. Thus Updike simultaneously demonstrates Rabbit's and our own contemporary loss of spiritual correspondences, our entrapment in the physical world.

With water as with the garden, Updike stresses the traditional religious connotations, only to show that they are no longer applicable. Rabbit's obsession with cleanliness, his repeated insistence that Ruth be washed before they make love, is our first indication that water has become a sign of our confinement to the human body, not an initiation into the body of Christ. Then, in the scene of the baby's drowning Updike takes care to elicit the traditional baptismal associations first, in which water is the connection between the physical and spiritual worlds. When the baby is at an age when infants are baptized, her mother "drops gently to her knees" to immerse the child in water. But the child is not "saved"; instead she dies. Water is the medium for physical death rather than spiritual life.

Finally, in each of Rabbit's three symbolic pilgrimages, by which he searches for some kind of spiritual revelation, Updike again follows this pattern of collapsing the religious expectations of both Rabbit and his reader. In the first section Rabbit and Ruth climb the mountain, in the second Rabbit goes to church, and in the third he again climbs the mountain, this time alone. In the first pilgrimage Updike evokes religious expectations by having

Rabbit and Ruth barefoot, climbing a mountain significantly named Mt. Judge, hoping to have a truth revealed at the top. But no vision is revealed, and Rabbit
turns to Ruth as though *she* were truth. With the visit
to church physical desires again intercede, making spiritual response impossible. And, at the end of the novel,
after his sense of religious certainty at the funeral, Rabbit finds the loneliness of the mountaintop too frighten-
ing, and so he flees.

The futility which these images convey is reinforced
by the secular imagery of the novel as well. Throughout,
there is an intricate interweaving of references to nets,
circles, and the holes in the middle of circles. The nets,
while evoking Rabbit's basketball past, convey his sense
of entrapment, captive of circumstances over which he
has no control. The circles allude to Rabbit's desperate
and ineffectual action in the novel, efforts to escape which
only return him to the same circumstances again and
again. The hole is the "emptiness at the center of the
circle" [3] (whether basketball goal, golf hole, or vagina),
a meaninglessness reflected in the dark church window.
All these images ultimately enclose rather than liberate;
they are meaningless in the sense that they do not lead
to a meaningfulness for Rabbit.

The drive that Rabbit takes when he first leaves
Janice is a microcosm of the futility and ambiguity
which both the religious and secular images convey. The
radio that Rabbit listens to as he drives gives forth a
mixture of the religious and the trivial, reflecting the
ambiguity in our society. The road signs are confusing
and misleading, often contradictory or even absent, as are
the directions which he will receive throughout the novel.
He does not know specifically where he is going, and
when he consults the authorities, maps and service sta-
tion attendants, they are no help. Finally Rabbit becomes
hopelessly lost, on "a road of horror" which is "a lover's
lane. In a hundred yards it ends." So will Rabbit find

himself, confused and directionless, driven into the en-
tanglements of sexual love, facing a dead end.

Thus the secular and religious imagery of the novel,
and its characters, combine to demonstrate its theme,
the confusion and uncertainty of contemporary society.
The feeling of uncertainty, of being faced with irreconcilable conflicts, is conveyed to the reader by Updike's
technical skill, so that our experience, as we read the
novel, mirrors Rabbit's. It forcefully reveals to us the
spiritual poverty of contemporary society and the dilemma
of man's dichotomy.

3

The Centaur

The Centaur, winner of the 1964 National Book Award and hailed by many critics as a minor masterpiece, is Updike's tribute to his father. Like the main character in the novel, Updike's father was a high school teacher who supported his son, his wife, and her parents for many years on a meager salary. The characterization of the father, mother, and grandfather, the concentration of all their hopes on their one, artistically talented son, even the farm outside of town where the family lives, all these aspects of the novel can be traced to Updike's past.

Updike has transformed this past into a mock epic,[1] a novel that rests upon the fundamental disjunction between classical allusions on a heroic scale and mundane events. The narrative of the novel moves back and forth from classical myth to literal realism in a way that may at first be confusing, but ultimately enriches the novel. The narrator, who presents the novel in this style, is Peter Caldwell, an artist living in Greenwich Village, who remembers the events of three days during his adolescence.

When Peter remembers his father in mythical terms he pictures him as the centaur Chiron. A centaur is a mythical demigod, with the upper body of a man and the lower body of a stallion. According to Greek myth, the centaur Chiron was accidentally wounded by a poisoned arrow and fated to suffer his pain endlessly because, like the gods, he was immortal. But when the gods needed a sacrifice to atone for the illegal theft of fire by Prometheus, Chiron begged to be chosen. He was accepted by the gods and died, thus liberating Prometheus, who had been chained to a rock by the gods after he stole their fire and gave it to mankind. In the context of the novel George Caldwell is Chiron, sacrificing himself for Peter Caldwell, the young Prometheus whose art will, they hope, bring light and fire to mankind.

The novel opens abruptly with mythical characters in a contemporary and realistic setting. Chiron, teaching a high school science class, is shot in the ankle with an arrow by one of his students. With the class laughing and jeering, Chiron leaves, painfully limping on his three remaining hooves to Hummel's Garage, where Al Hummel (Vulcan) removes the arrow with a butane torch. Returning to the high school, Chiron hobbles to his classroom by the circuitous basement route to avoid the principal's office. In the basement he remembers encountering Vera Hummel, Al Hummel's attractive and sensuous wife, in the girls' locker room. As Venus, she scorns yet desires the half-stallion, but the centaur refuses her advances, worried that the principal, Zimmerman (Zeus), will discover them.

Returning to his classroom, Chiron finds that Zimmerman has taken over the class in his absence. Refusing to hear Chiron's explanation, the principal remains to evaluate his teaching. Caldwell/Chiron proceeds to conduct a class on the scientific explanation of the creation of the universe. But he loses control of the class; the students grow increasingly restive, and the teacher finally hits one of them amid the chaos.

The next chapter is written in entirely realistic terms, without overt reference to myth. As it opens fifteen-year-old Peter Caldwell remembers lying in bed one wintry morning in 1947; he overhears his father tell his mother

of his fear that he has some fatal illness. Slipping into
a daydream, the adolescent Peter imagines sex with his
girl friend, until he is routed from bed by his mother's
command. As he dresses he observes his psoriasis, a skin
condition that covers his chest and arms with thick scabs,
a secret curse that he hides from others. Amid admoni-
tions and recriminations from the mother, with advice
faintly offered in the background by the grandfather,
George and Peter hurriedly leave for school in their old
black Buick, formerly a hearse. On the way to school
George picks up a hitchhiking tramp whom he drives
miles out of their way so that both father and son are
late for their first class.

This literal story is interrupted by a short chapter
during which Chiron is pictured as teaching his students
the mythical theory of creation. Then in chapter 4 we
return to the realistic mode, after school the same day.
Peter first meets his girl friend at the teenage hangout,
then goes to the doctor's office where his father, still
suspecting a fatal illness, is having a thorough examination. The doctor takes x-rays and advises Caldwell to
"Get rest and don't think."

That evening Peter and his father, who is coach of
the high school swim team, go to a swim meet at which
the Olinger team is badly beaten. When Peter and his
father get in the car to go home, it won't start. As they
walk to a hotel, they are confronted by a drunk who
assumes the older man is seducing the adolescent boy
and demands money as a payoff not to tell the police.
Caldwell sympathetically gives him his last thirty-five
cents. He takes a room in a cheap hotel (paying by
check), where father and son spend the night. They return to their classes at the high school next morning,
arranging for Al Hummel to fix the car.

Chapters 5 and 6 interrupt the realistic narrative
with, first, a newspaper-style obituary for George Caldwell, praising his "more-than-human selflessness." Then

Peter is envisaged as Prometheus, tied to a rock, visited by friends, tormented by sexual fantasies and guilt over his father's suffering on his behalf.

Chapter 7 returns to the realistic narrative, beginning by focusing on George Caldwell's worries: his suspicions of a fatal illness, his son's future, his debts, the farm he is unwillingly saddled with, the principal who may fire him, the students who drain him of his energy, the car that does not work, the care of his old father-in-law, the pain in his teeth. After finishing another day at school he goes to the dentist to have a rotten tooth pulled.

At the high school basketball game that evening, George admires Vera Hummel from a distance, while Peter flirts with his girl friend, later revealing to her his secret psoriasis and embracing her. Meanwhile his father questions a Reformed Church minister (at the basketball game with a Sunday school class) for clarification of some theological concerns. But the clergyman is too busy flirting with Vera/Venus to listen.

After the game, Peter and his father attempt to drive home in a severe snowstorm, but the car gets stuck several miles out of town. Walking back to town in the blustering snow and freezing cold, Peter recalls his father urging him on and putting his own hat on Peter's head.

In chapter 8 Peter remembers waking in the Hummel's guest bedroom, having staggered there with his father in the storm the night before. He spends the morning alone with Vera Hummel, entranced with her sensuality, daydreaming of intimacies with her. When his father arrives from school, cancelled because of the storm, Al Hummel drives father and son to their car and helps them dig it out of the snow. Peter and his father finally drive home, stopping on the way for groceries and walking the last half-mile, since the road is unplowed. Their homecoming is happy; Peter's mother greets them as heroes, Peter's grandfather is well, and the doctor has called to report that George's x-rays showed nothing. Peter, with a fever and cold, goes to bed. The next morning, he watches his father through the bedroom window leaving alone, in the cold and snow, to teach school.

The final short chapter returns to the mythical vision. It describes Chiron, walking through the winter landscape to his car, the former hearse. He takes comfort in the thought that the x-rays were clear, enabling him to sustain his family a little longer. He sees the hearse and understands it as a chariot from Zimmerman/Zeus, calling him to a kind of death. He accepts that death in the final sentence of the novel.

George Caldwell dies spiritually, not physically, at the end of *The Centaur*. Updike has told us that *The Centaur* says "yes to self-sacrifice and duty, but—what of a man's private agony and dwindling?" [2] When George Caldwell goes off to face again the painful pressures of his job in order to provide for his family, he walks toward a hearse that carries him to the spiritually suffocating atmosphere, the hellish environment, of the high school. The very image of a centaur, half one thing and half another, pictures graphically man's painful duality. But the godlike "Chiron" dies at the end of the novel. George Caldwell lives on, having sacrificed his spiritual fulfillment to the demands of the community he lives in.

In his science lecture to the class in the opening chapter of the novel, Caldwell singles out the volvox for special attention in the evolutionary process. "While each cell is potentially immortal," he tells the students, "by volunteering for a specialized function within an organized society of cells, the volvox enters a compromised environment. The strain eventually wears it out and kills it. It dies sacrificially, for the good of the whole." Like the volvox, George Caldwell gives up his life "for the good of the whole." [3]

Constantly belittling himself, always sympathetic and obliging to others, George Caldwell is willing to sacrifice himself to everyone in the community, even total strangers. He picks up a forlorn hitchhiker and drives miles out of his way to take him to his destination. When he discovers the tramp has stolen his gloves, George tells Peter that the "poor devil" no doubt "needs 'em more than I did." He sympathetically tells an anxious student the answers to a forthcoming test. He alone applauds a swimmer who has performed poorly. He gives an insulting drunk his last handful of change, saying, "I'd like to give you more, my friend, but I just don't have it."

As Peter's provider, George worries constantly about his son, fearing that he is an inadequate father, fearing even more that he will die and leave the boy fatherless, indulging him with movies, hamburgers, and shakes they can ill afford. The scene in which, walking through the storm, George puts his own hat on Peter's head is representative.

George even sustains his father-in-law and the steadfast Christian faith that he, alone in the novel, represents. Grandfather Kramer ritualistically calls blessings on each family member at bedtime or at their departure. He lives on nothing but bread, putting whole slices into his toothless mouth as if he were simultaneously feeding his body and the Christian faith for which bread is the symbol of nourishment. George Caldwell believes his role is to bring the bread that keeps this faith alive. At the grocery store where they stop before finally arriving home after three days' absence, George buys bread for the old man.

Although he nourishes the grandfather's faith and perhaps envies it, George Caldwell cannot himself endorse it. Two clocks hang in the farmhouse, and George, significantly, tells time by a different clock than the grandfather. George's clock is modern and accelerated, just as Caldwell lives at an accelerated pace, always rushing, always late, always seeing death as imminent. The grandfather's clock is old and slow, a family heirloom, past its present usefulness.

George cannot forget that his own father, a minister, despaired at the moment of death when he needed faith most. Caldwell tries to believe what he was taught as a child: "I was a minister's son. I was brought up to believe, and I shall believe it, that God made man as the last best thing in His Creation." But in the same breath he goes on to question time's power over man and his faith: "If that's the case, who are this time and tide who are so almighty superior to us?" Thus he tells the minister at the basketball game that the only thing he sees as infinite about God's mercy is its infinite distance.

Turning from the Christian faith that for his generation does not live, George Caldwell is left with the belief that "Only goodness lives. But it does live." Thus his obituary describes George as having a "more than human selflessness," and, indeed, this novel is Updike's most affirmative statement of dedication to good works. But this altruism exacts a terrible price—the sacrifice of spirit.

Resisting the sacrifice that will ultimately be demanded of him, George Caldwell translates all spiritual frustration into physical suffering. Thus his body becomes a cursed burden that imprisons the spirit. There is a sense in which he wishes for the physical death that eludes him. Doc Appleton recognizes George's problematic duality when he tells him that all his tension develops from the fact that "You believe in the soul. You believe your body is like a horse you get up on and ride for a while and then get off. You ride your body too hard. You show it no love. This is not natural."

Like all other Updike dentists and doctors, Doc Appleton
concentrates on the body to the exclusion of the soul. He
believes in nothing and belongs to no church. According
to him mankind has made two mistakes: "one was to
stand up and the other was to start thinking. It strains
the spine and the nerves."

When Doc Appleton tells George that his trouble is
"you have never come to terms with your own body," the
teacher answers, "You're right . . . I hate the damn
ugly thing." As pressures increase, George "by searching
through his body can uncover any color and shape of
pain he wants," from toothache to ingrown toenail. It is
implied that even sex gives George no bodily pleasure;
he refuses Vera Hummel, and his wife hints that he is
"a man who hates sex."

On the other hand, Peter, both as adolescent and
mature narrator, is preoccupied with his body. Peter's
idol is a high school friend named Dedman, who is always
flashing pornographic playing cards; his very name hints
at the consequences of carnal obsession. During the high
school basketball game, while his father is questioning
the minister, Peter kneels before his girl friend. In this
act of sexual worship the final futility of directing rever-
ence to such an object is indicated when Peter discovers
that "where her legs meet there is nothing. . . . This
then is the secret the world holds at its center, this
innocence, this absence. . . ." This act initiates him into
the house of Venus (Vera Hummel), and as he walks
home with his father at the end of the novel Peter asks
whether you can steer by the star Venus. His father
responds, "I don't know. I've never tried. It's an inter-
esting question."

Peter's growing concentration on the natural, physical world is reflected in his gradual loss of the supernatural, mythical vision during the course of the novel.
Peter's initial perception of his father as Chiron reflects
the son's tendency to make his father godlike, to make

of him a myth. In reference to his use of myth in
The Centaur Updike has said, "there is a way in which,
to a child, everything is myth size." [4] Certainly Peter
idolizes his father; he writes, "to me, my father seemed
changeless." His father's face seems, to the boy, "half-
way to the sky," and "nothing could ever go wrong" in
his presence.

But clashing with this mythical vision is the adolescent Peter's opposing tendency to see his father as bum-
bling, ineffectual, and ridiculous. In these literal and
often critical passages Peter looks at his father objectively
and dispassionately, that is, without myth. He fears that
his father's unselfish actions make him the object of
ridicule. For, according to Peter, none of the people
whom his father helps are worthy, and all his father's
sacrifices seem to his son "mediocre, fruitless, cloying
involvement."

These two opposing views create the mixture of myth
and literal realism that the novel incorporates. The
death of Chiron at the end of the novel not only indicates
George Caldwell's spiritual resignation to the demands of
this world, but it also signifies the collapse of the mythical vision for Peter Caldwell. In other words, Peter Caldwell's perception of his father as Chiron dies, taking with
it his metaphoric vision. While *The Centaur* begins with
Peter's profession of his father's similarity to the gods,
it ends with his loss of it, and of the entire mythical framework that it sustained.

This loss of the narrator's mythical vision and his
adoption of a philosophy of naturalism in its stead is conveyed in our last glimpse of Peter in the novel. He is in
bed, ill with a cold, watching his father walk to the car
from his bedroom window. It is, appropriately, only after
his father is lost to his sight that Peter formulates his
philosophy of naturalism. He begins by recognizing the
tension between the real and the mythical, but now there
is uncertainty in his mind concerning the heroic, or

mythical, or metaphoric significance of the scene he has pictured:

I knew what this scene was—a patch of Pennsylvania in 1947—and yet I did not know, was in my softly fevered state mindlessly soaked in a rectangle of colored light. I burned to paint it, just like that, in its puzzle of glory; it came upon me that I must go to Nature disarmed of perspective and stretch myself like a large transparent canvas upon her in the hope that, my submission being perfect, the imprint of a beautiful and useful truth would be taken.

What Peter Caldwell knows is the empirical evidence, the historical factuality of the scene. What he does not know is its metaphoric meaning. Yet he decides that the way to represent that scene artistically is to "go to Nature disarmed of perspective," to try to capture meaning without metaphor, and attempt to become the object, rather than interpret it. He will submit himself to earth, to Nature, abandoning metaphoric perspectives, in an attempt to reach "a beautiful and useful truth."

So it is that Peter has become, in his own words, "an authentic second-rate abstract expressionist" living with a Negro mistress who represents to him a kind of sensuality. As the young Prometheus, for whom his father gave up his life, Peter's artistic talent had seemed worthy of such a sacrifice. From the first the child believed that in his art he could fix time and achieve a victory over death. When confronted in the museum or at 4-H Club meetings with the mortality of the animal world, the child would immediately immerse himself in art, suspending and escaping natural law.

But the adult narrator, committed to "abstract expressionism," is beginning to doubt whether such a purely personal art can suspend time or reach eternal truths. Peter is no longer Prometheus. The metaphoric vacuum of expressionism has led him to "earnestly bloated canvasses I conscientiously cover with great streaks" that are "straining to say . . . the unsayable thing, and I grow frightened." Having become an atheist, a sensualist, and an expressionist in his art, Peter is beginning to realize that without the metaphoric vision, without myth, art is impossible. Confined to the literal and natural world, lacking the symbolic vision that transforms it, Peter Caldwell has become, as he himself admits, a failure.

Thus, in this novel, Peter Caldwell demonstrates the artist's need for a framework of belief, a mythical vision, whether Christian or classical. *The Centaur* is Peter Caldwell's recognition of this need, and his attempt to recapture the mythical vision of his childhood. He remembers his whole family as living "on a firm stage, resonant with metaphor. . . . We lived in God's sight." But the adult can recapture this sense of metaphor, this heroic vision, only intermittently, and this psychological fact accounts for the mixture of myth and literal reality in the novel.

Thus, I am suggesting that *The Centaur* tells not one story, but two. First and most obviously, *The Centaur* is about the father, George Caldwell, whose Christian faith is so full of doubt that all he has left of Christian dogma is ethical action. To this he devotes himself so selflessly that he sacrifices his own desire for fulfillment, giving his life to his family and his community.

But the mixture of myth and literal reality in the telling of this first story reveals a second story, concerning Peter Caldwell, the adult narrator of the novel. The heroic scale shows the veneration that the child attaches to the father, making him almost a god, and the inflated value that we place on mundane events when we are adolescents. The interruption of the heroic with the factual reveals the adolescent's growing awareness of literal reality and the fallibility of his parents. The adult narrator, a failed artist, looks back nostalgically and attempts to recapture the heroic metaphor of his childhood.

He succeeds only intermittently. Thus, while Updike demonstrates the dependence of the artist upon a mythical framework, he simultaneously shows the impossibility of completely resurrecting that mythical framework in a contemporary world that concentrates on factual reality. In *The Centaur* Peter Caldwell's attempt to recapture a mythical perception into which he can put the events of the past is interrupted by the factual realism that counterpoints the heroic vision throughout the novel. Yet the heroic metaphor is maintained sufficiently for him to create a work of art that is, though not heroic, mock heroic.

The epigraph to *The Centaur* is a quotation from the theologian Karl Barth: "Heaven is the creation inconceivable to man, earth the creation conceivable to him. He himself is the creature on the boundary between heaven and earth." The painful dichotomy of such a creature, whose spirit attempts to reach heaven through myth, whose body is tied mortally to earth, is revealed in the image of the suffering centaur. It is also revealed by his son, who, when he abandons myth and devotes himself to the natural, relinquishing heaven for earth, loses the tension that makes art possible. He is hounded by bad dreams and a sense of unworthiness and guilt over the sacrifices made for him by his father. It is the inevitable result of Updike's belief that "without the supernatural, the natural is a pit of horror." [5]

4

Of the Farm

The shortest of Updike's novels, *Of the Farm* may also be
the most evocative. The lyrical descriptions of the sensual
and the pastoral contrast dramatically with the bitter, ac-
cusatory, quarrelsome conversations that permeate the
novel. Thus the poetic simplicity of the natural and sensual is opposed to the complicated and tense entanglement
of human relationships among the characters. The dramatic effect of the novel is heightened by its limitation,
for the most part, to one setting, its compression into
forty-eight hours, and its exclusive focus on four characters.

The overt action of the novel can be summarized
quickly. Late Friday afternoon Joey Robinson, his new
wife, Peggy, and her eleven-year-old son by her first marriage arrive at the farm where Joey's mother lives alone.
They eat dinner. Peggy and Mrs. Robinson wash up, they
go to bed, Peggy and Joey make love. The next day Joey
mows the field that lies fallow beside the farm, his
mother being too old and ill to do it herself. After lunch
they go to the market, and then Joey returns to his mowing until he is interrupted by a storm in the late afternoon.

The next day, Sunday, Joey and his mother go to
church where they hear a sermon about Adam and Eve.
On the way home, Mrs. Robinson is stricken by an at-

tack, for she suffers from both angina and emphysema. The doctor recommends hospitalization, but Mrs. Robinson won't leave her farm. Although Joey offers to stay, Mrs. Robinson insists that he leave with his new family as scheduled Sunday afternoon.

The tense conversations that embellish these spare actions circle and recircle issues in the Robinsons' past, interpreting and reinterpreting, excusing and accusing, occasionally revealing conciliatory gestures that recognize the possible validity of another's point of view. Underneath all of these conversations the reader senses the emotional control of the mother over her son, the jealous rivalry over Joey between his mother and his wife, the desperate loneliness of the sick old woman who lives alone on a remote farm, and the bewilderment of the new wife who sees her husband, during the course of a weekend, withdraw from her. Finally, the first-person narration conveys to us the feelings of guilt, the defensiveness, and the profound uncertainty of Joey Robinson, who has left his first wife and three children to marry Peggy and who needs, but does not expect, his mother's approval. The entire novel is told from Joey's point of view, and we see him dominated alternately by his mother and his new wife, to whom he goes for such complete immersion in sensuality that he is able to forget, temporarily, the anxieties that burden him.

When we first meet Joey's mother, we begin to understand his anxieties. Mrs. Robinson dresses in a man's sweater as she has, all her life, appropriated the dominant role traditionally assigned to the male. Years before, she moved her father, her husband, and her son, all unwilling, to the farm where she still lives. She has loved only two things in her life: her son and her farm. She has lost the one to a new wife, and her failing health implies that she will soon lose the other. Throughout the novel she attempts to win her son back from his wife and guarantee that he will keep the farm, even after she dies. Because she loves the farm with deep devotion, for Joey to sell it would be, she feels, a betrayal.

When Joey first enters the farmhouse he enters an environment that clashes jarringly with the present. The farmhouse is alive with the presence of Joey's father, dead now for a year. On the first night there Joey writes, "I listened for his footstep to scuff on the porch." Joey imagines his father looking at him "with his mixture of mischief and sorrow," greeting him fondly. Joey puts on his father's old dungarees to mow and uses his father's razor, revealing both his nostalgia for the father and his unconscious, oedipal desire to be his mother's lover.

On the farmhouse walls hang pictures of Joey's childhood and graduation, reminders that he has not fulfilled his mother's earlier hopes for him. His mother had wanted Joey to be "a poet, like Wordsworth," and had sent him to Harvard because of its impressive record in producing great poets. Instead, Joey now has what Mrs. Robinson calls a "prostitute's job" as an advertising executive.

But the pictures on the farmhouse walls that disturb Joey even more deeply are those of his first wife, Joan, and their children. The photo of Joey "clowning in the sun" with his children and another of Joan, through which he perceives her "natural grace," arouse feelings of guilt and a wistfulness that touches on regret. As if the photos were not enough, Mrs. Robinson often leads the conversation toward the rejected wife and her children. Disappointed with his divorce and remarriage, she speaks sympathetically of the cast-off wife and reminisces about her grandchildren, lamenting that she will never see them again.

Joey retaliates by accusing his mother of being partly responsible for the breakup of his marriage. He asks her, "Why did you dislike Joan so much? In the end you made me dislike her." But his mother's references to his ex-wife and children, and the photographs, open up Joey's just recently buried feelings of guilt, so that he dreams that his little boy has become stunted and misshapen and thinks of his children often, with regret.

Jealous of her son's new wife, Mrs. Robinson bluntly criticizes Peggy in her private conversations with Joey. She accuses Peggy of being "vulgar" and "stupid," and she tells her son that she is surprised "that you would need a stupid woman to give you confidence." Peggy has expensive tastes and will be such a financial drain on Joey that Mrs. Robinson wonders whether he can afford to continue sending her a small monthly check. Mrs. Robinson bitterly predicts that after her death Peggy will convince Joey to sell the farm in order to support her costly habits.

His mother evokes such resentment and emotion in Joey that after their conversation on Friday night he goes upstairs to Peggy, trembling. He tells her, "I'm thirty-five and I've been through hell and I don't see why that old lady has to have such a hold over me. It's ridiculous. It's degrading." Peggy comforts him with lovemaking, but during the course of the weekend she senses Mrs. Robinson's increasing control over Joey.

Peggy retailiates, telling her mother-in-law that she's the only woman Joey has "ever met who was willing to let him be a man." She insinuates that she will be a better wife for Joey than Mrs. Robinson was for Joey's father. "Peggy's idea," Joey tells us, "was that my mother had undervalued and destroyed my father, had been inadequately a 'woman' to him, had brought him to a farm which was in fact her giant lover. . . ."

Peggy's eleven-year-old son, Richard, also becomes a battlefield between the two women. He quickly develops an attachment to the old lady, and Peggy, perhaps jealous, becomes possessive and tells her mother-in-law, "He's not going to be another Joey." In response to this accusation, Joey tells us,

My mother turned to me, as if to her historian, and said, "She takes my grandchildren from me, she turns my son into a gray-haired namby-pamby, and now she won't let me show this poor disturbed child a little affection, which he badly needs."

It is true that in the novel, Peggy is less affectionate and concerned about Richard than is Joey, who is, after all, not even the boy's father. Peggy is concentrating all her attention, at this time, on her marriage, but it shows strain nonetheless.

Under his mother's influence, Joey becomes increasingly critical of Peggy and jealous and suspicious of her first husband and former lovers. He admits, to his mother, that Peggy is "vulgar" and "stupid," and that he made a mistake in divorcing Joan and marrying Peggy. He tells his mother that he loves Joan now: "It's amazing how much I love her, now that she's in Canada." But after these admissions late Saturday night, Mrs. Robinson sends her son upstairs to bed, so as not to "keep Peggy waiting any longer," and he goes obediently into Peggy's welcoming arms.

After the sermon on Sunday, in which females are defined as sensual and derivative, and after her emphysema attack the same morning, Mrs. Robinson makes a tentative peace with Peggy, accepting her son's new marriage. Joey considers staying on at the farm alone with his mother, looking after her until she is well, but Mrs. Robinson insists "I want you all to go back to New York where you belong." She promises that "the next time they come," she will get a photo of Peggy, so that she too will be memorialized on the farmhouse walls, accepted as part of the family. She and Peggy agree that Joey is "a good boy," and Joey, in turn, talks of the farm as "ours," his and his mother's, accepting responsibility for it should his mother die.

Updike has said that in *Of the Farm* "the mythical

has fled the ethical." [1] In other words, in this short novel
the mythical or supernatural has disappeared, leaving us
exclusively with ethical action in the physical or natural
world. *Of the Farm* is also Updike's first novel in which
the male protagonist has entirely succumbed to the domination of women. These two facts, at first glance seemingly unrelated, are in fact intimately connected. In Updike's novels, the domination of women brings about the
loss of supernatural yearning and the myth by which it
seeks expression.

Generally, Updike's women do not have that spiritual
need that his male characters express in their mythical beliefs. Almost all of his female characters lack that difficult dichotomy, that tense opposition between body and
spirit, that attraction toward the supernatural, that Updike's male protagonists feel. His female characters are
primarily physical. They are closer to the world of nature
and more comfortable with their physicality, their own
natural drives and impulses, than the male characters.

Since Updike's women seldom feel the spiritual
searching, the need for myth, that his men are constantly
attempting to realize, the domination of women in *Of
the Farm* implies the reduction of the mythical to the
merely ethical. The minister in *Of the Farm* says that by
accepting Eve, Adam "ties himself ethically to the
earth." The domination of Updike's women over men
brings about the male's rejection of his spirituality and
the religion, or myth, by which it seeks expression. The
dominated male abandons his yearning for another world
through the combined force of his partial, and the
woman's total, physicality. The relationships men form
with women commit them to that physical world that
women represent to Updike.

Thus, desire for women is at once the barrier to
spiritual fulfillment and the means to physical fulfillment
in men. As the sermon in *Of the Farm* puts it:

Man, with Woman's creation, became confused as to where to turn. With one half of his being he turns toward her, his rib, as if into himself, into the visceral and nostalgic warmth wherein his tensions find *re*solution in *dis*solution. With his other half he gazes outward, toward God, along the straight line of infinity. He seeks to *solve* the riddle of his death. Eve does not.

By dividing man in half, one half attracted to women, the other half gazing "outward toward God," the minister has emphasized the duality we have seen operating throughout Updike's fiction, and he has indicated that women belong on the side of the body, not the soul.

Because he is dominated by women, Joey Robinson is, in a sense, half a man, the half that is concerned with the ethical rather than the mythical, the natural rather than the supernatural. Perhaps this is why his mother and his wife agree, at the end of the novel, that he is "a good boy" rather than a man.

Joey's preoccupation with the physical world is concentrated in the body of his new wife. He views his wife's skirt, as she walks in front of him, as a "glimmering breadth . . . the center, the seat, of my life." And Peggy reciprocates by identifying herself totally with Joey's attention so that if he were to abandon her, she "saw herself abolished." Her identity, then, is entirely dependent on physical love; "Love my cunt, love me," she tells Joey. She believes in no god, but in "women giving themselves to men, of men in return giving women a reason to live." In this arrangement she is as dependent on him as he is on her, but for Joey it is perfect. He is dominated by a dependent woman.

That Joey finds Peggy's corrections of him "precious" is evidence of this need to be dominated. One of his former wife's faults was that she did not criticize him. Although he agrees with his mother that Peggy is stupid and vulgar, Joey is proud of her. He wonders, however, whether it was necessary for him to marry Peggy;

he wonders whether he could have "retained her, as mistress, *as long as her beauty lasted,* while remaining married to Joan" (italics mine), and his qualification tells us that it is not Peggy's mind, whether stupid or not, that concerns him.

Peggy's body is, for Joey, a substitute for the farm his mother loves. "My wife is a field," he tells us, which "entered . . . yields a variety of landscapes, seeming now a rolling perspective of bursting cotton balls . . . now a taut vista of mesas . . . now a gray French castle . . . now something like Antarctica; and then a receding valleyland of blacks and purples." This is indeed Joey's reduced world in which the freedom to be entirely immersed in physicality is "a pull more serious than that of gravity."

Joey traces his complete dedication to the body of his wife, and its consequences, in a bedtime story he tells Richard. The story is about a frog who is very small inside his body, who spears flies (at this point Joey thinks of "poor Joan"), but who finally disappears somewhere "deep in the dungeon of his guts" where he is searching for treasure; "the lower he went the smaller he got, until finally, just when he was sure he had reached the dungeon where the treasure was, he disappeared!" The disappearance is, of course, the loss of duality, the death of the spirit, inevitable when the total being is devoted to a search for sexual "treasure."

Joey's mother's "giant lover" is the farm, making hers a broader, but still earthbound, vision. Joey's allegiance wavers between the old farm, the pastoral ideal that his mother wishes him to maintain, and the body of his wife, his new farm. Committed to either Peggy or his mother, Joey is committed to the earth. He finally must choose his wife's body over the old farm, simply because, for him, and all of Updike's male protagonists, nature means death. Mrs. Robinson's farm has depressed all the males in her family—her father, her husband, and her son.

While Nature means death to the men, for women it means the preservation of life. In their relations with the world of external nature women express their mothering or nurturing impulse. As the sermon says, "Her very name, *Hava,* means 'living.' Her motherhood answers concretely what men would answer abstractly." Thus, in mowing the field, Joey imitates war, for he feels the physical world as a threat to his potential spirituality, while Mrs. Robinson imitates love, embracing the field around its perimeter. Joey, linking the fatal and the sexual as all Updike's male protagonists do, is "excited by destruction" of the physical world. Joey's destruction of the field does bring death, it fails to spare the pheasant's nest or the wild flowers that his mother lifts the cutter for. His mother preserves nature, saving doomed dogs, watering flowers, and scattering seed for the birds, as does Peggy.

Mrs. Robinson's devotion to the natural world brings with it the loss of the mythical, or supernatural, in her beliefs. The farm to which she has devoted her life represents her only hope of immortality. In its preservation by Joey, she will somehow be preserved. Thus, she tries to make Joey promise to keep the farm after her death, yet unhappily predicts its being parceled out to make way for a subdivision, so that Joey can support Peggy's expensive tastes.

While Mrs. Robinson is nominally a Christian, her God is not the abstract, supernatural being whose belief necessitates faith. Instead, the natural world, perceived by the senses, is her "God." "I believe only in what I can see or touch," Mrs. Robinson tells Richard, affirming women's essential physicality. "I see and touch God all the time. . . . If I couldn't see and touch Him here on the farm, if I lived in New York City, I don't know if I'd believe or not." To Joey his mother's "religiosity seems unaccompanied by belief." It is merely ethical action, adherence to the customs of going to church and not letting Joey mow on Sundays.

Peggy's complete dedication to sensuality allows for no religious faith at all. And while his new wife's "un-thinking non-Christianity" sometimes worries Joey, it does not bother him enough to teach Richard a bedtime prayer. Although Joey does go to church on Sunday morning with his mother, the most affirmative statement he can make about his belief is the doubly qualified "I think I meant that I believed."

"Kindness needs no belief," the minister in his ser-mon tells us; in the absence of the mythical, the novel concentrates on the ethical action, the kindness, that the main characters attempt to compromise with their own selfish desires. Updike has said that *Of the Farm* is about "moral readjustment," [2] and that "the underlying the-matic transaction, as I conceived it, was the mutual for-giveness of mother and son, the acceptance each of the other's guilt in taking what they had wanted, to the dis-comfort, respectively, of the dead father and the divorced wife." [3] So the ethical without a mythical framework be-comes a matter of moral readjustment in which ethical action is less apparent than the guilt that accompanies the failure to act ethically. Joey's and his mother's guilt ac-cumulates because they have betrayed their ethical re-sponsibilities in their relations to their families. The mother's purchase of the farm alienated her husband and child. The son's devotion to *his* farm, Peggy, obviously meant the casting off of first wife and children. But the mother's willingness to put a photograph of Peggy on the wall and the son's acceptance of mutual ownership of the farm at the end of the novel does represent a step toward "mutual forgiveness."

Joey and his dead father believed that "Women made the rules, women made the babies, women did every-thing." This control of men by women, combined with the fact that women "don't understand about the stars," reduces the male, limiting his vision.

There is no doubt that Updike consistently presents women as limited and sensual, a threat to man's spiritual vision. At the same time they, and the earth to which they are so inextricably linked, provide the inspiration for Updike's most lyrical prose. It is finally this quality of poetic lyricism that I find most memorable in *Of the Farm*. Updike's description of Joey's mowing is a superb example of sustained lyricism:

Swallows. gathering in the fleeting insects, flicked around me, as gulls escort a ship. . . . Stretched scatterings of flowers moved in a piece, like the heavens, constellated by my wheel's revolution, on my right; and lay as drying fodder on my left. . . . Crickets sprang crackling away from the wheels; butterflies loped through their tumbling universe and bobbed above the flattened grass. . . .

The lyricism is equally evocative when Joey describes, in sensual terms, his wife's naked body: "My wife is wide, wide-hipped and long-waisted, and surveyed from above, gives an impression of terrain, of a wealth whose ownership imposes upon my own body a sweet strain of extension. . . ." Or consider the poetic resonance of Joey's boyhood memory of his mother: "I seemed to be in bed, and a tall girl stood over me, and her hair came loose from her shoulder and fell forward filling the air with a swift liquid motion, and hung there, as a wing edged with light, and enclosed me in a tent as she bent lower to deliver her good-night kiss." It is this kind of writing that has led critics to describe Updike as having an unmatched gift for language.

5

Couples

The publication of *Couples* in 1968 caused a small sensation. It launched Updike onto the best-seller list for almost a year. It made his name, if not a household word, at least far more familiar to a reading public that had formerly been fairly exclusive. The public read the novel avidly, probably as much because of its sexual detail as for its literary merit. Most critics were less enthusiastic, primarily because they felt Updike had sold out to cheap sensationalism, squandering his literary talents on an unworthy subject. They failed to recognize Updike's serious purpose in the novel.

Updike has told us that *Couples* is "about sex as the emergent religion," [1] and indeed, it chronicles as effectively as any twentieth-century novel the near-worship of sex in contemporary American society, and its consequences. While I feel that the novel would be more successful if it were condensed, I also feel that no other novel presents mid-twentieth-century American suburban sexuality, its practice and its consequences, so effectively.

The novel is set in a fictitious New England town, Tarbox, Massachusetts, close enough to Boston to be a "bedroom community." Updike focuses on ten white, middle-class couples, most of them with children, houses, mortgages, and professional occupations. Piet Hanema is the protagonist, a thirty-five-year-old building contractor who, at the beginning of the novel, is having an affair with Georgene Thorne. Part of Georgene's attraction for Piet is that, in taking her as mistress, he insults her husband, Freddy Thorne, the main antagonist of the novel and spokesman for the new sex-obsessed life-style of the couples in Tarbox.

Piet and Freddy represent the major conflict of the novel. While Piet is full of religious doubt, he attends church regularly in a futile attempt to hold on to his faith. Piet has never recovered from the shock of his parents' accidental death years before. Haunted by the possibility of death without immortal life, Piet desperately attempts to pray; he struggles through long dark nights with insomnia induced by his fear of death. He is married to Angela, a serenely untroubled woman who accepts death as part of the natural cycle and who thus cannot understand her husband's fears. But other women, sensing the desperation in Piet, find him attractive, and he turns to them as the possible solution to his anxieties.

Freddy Thorne, on the other hand, glories in the passing of the old religion and has designated himself high priest of sensuality. He believes that since man lacks a spirit, he should devote his life to enjoying his body in sexual abandonment, accepting the death that will ultimately come to it.

The newcomers to the community are Ken Whitman, a research biologist, and his pregnant wife, Foxy. Ken's calculating scientific rationality has always caused a lack of communication in their marriage. When they hire Piet to renovate their house, he finds Foxy's nurturing and pregnant state irresistible. Their affair allays Piet's fear of death; Foxy is religious and procreative in contrast to Angela, who does not go to church and refuses to have more children.

After her son by Ken is born, Foxy gets pregnant by Piet, and he goes to Freddy Thorne, who arranges an abortion. Freddy's price is a night with Angela, during which he is impotent. But Foxy's husband, who has been unaware of the affair, is informed of it by Georgene Thorne, who is jealous of Piet's attachment to Foxy. Ken and Foxy separate, as do Angela and Piet. Soon after, the church Piet had so faithfully attended symbolically burns down. His loss of the spiritual quest culminates in his marriage to Foxy, who has become his new, but much diminished, religion.

Like all résumés, this summary leaves out many particulars and is an injustice to the complexity of the novel. For example, I have not detailed the frequent gatherings of the entire group of Tarbox couples, their basketball games, their parties involving dancing, word games, drinking, and flirting. Nor have I mentioned Piet's other affairs during the course of the novel. Finally, I have left out a whole chapter, "Applesmiths and Other Games," which focuses not on Piet and Foxy but on the double affair between the Applebys and the Smiths. The effect of these enlargements from an exclusive concentration on Piet and Foxy is to create a whole community devoted to a way of life about which Updike has serious doubts, but which he seems to believe is being embraced in contemporary middle-class America.

In the *Time* feature story that closely followed the publication of *Couples* Updike said: "There's a lot of dry talk around about love and sex being somehow the ground of our morality. . . . I thought I should describe the ground and ask, is it entirely to be wished for?" [2] The reader of *Couples* may feel some confusion in his attempt to answer that question. Certainly Updike has successfully posed the question: sex and physical love are shown throughout the novel as the "new ground of our morality." But is Updike suggesting that it *is* or *isn't* "entirely to be wished for?" Does he criticize sex as "the emergent religion," or does he sympathize with and even celebrate the new hedonism?

It is my belief that, in *Couples,* Updike both criticizes and celebrates the new sexual standards. The main

story line of the novel, involving Piet, portrays the celebration of sex. Piet's gradual acceptance of sex as the
emergent religion, his relinquishment of Christian hopes,
or more correctly fears, is treated seriously and sympathetically by Updike. Piet's affair with Foxy is the celebration of sexual love as the most profound, the closest
to the religious, of all natural experiences.

Yet sex remains an experience within this world, a
natural rather than a supernatural experience. It is from
this awareness of the inadequacy of sex as a religion,
from the disappointed hope for the supernatural, that Updike has infused parts of *Couples* with satire. Thus Freddy
Thorne and some of the minor characters in the novel are
deliberately satirical. Updike uses them to criticize "sex as
the emergent religion."

Updike admitted the presence of these two attitudes
when he commented that there is a "no, in *Couples*, to a
religious community founded on physical and psychical
interpretation, but—what else shall we do, as God destroys our churches?" [3] Updike's "no" is conveyed
largely through the satirical element in the novel, while
his "but" is conveyed through the sympathetic celebration
of Piet.

For Updike's treatment of Piet is consistently compas-
sionate. He presents his protagonist as a victim of his
time. The contemporary church fails to fulfill his spiritual
needs; the preacher in the novel is more concerned with
material than spiritual matters. Yet Updike is aware
that Piet's final substitution of sexual and earthly love is
an inadequate answer to spiritual needs.

Piet begins, then, as a victim of his own duality, of
his desire for something more than the natural world, for
a belief that would calm the fears of the body's death in
this world. When prayer works for Piet, "His existence
for a second seemed to evade decay." But prayer works
infrequently at the beginning, and never toward the end
of the novel. He has dreams from which he awakens "con-

vinced of his death," and prayer fails to dispel his fear. His only comfort is in thinking of Foxy: "She believed. She adored his prick."

In one scene he becomes so terrified by mortality that his thoughts become a litany of death. This is one of the most powerful moments in the novel: "Revolving terror scooped the shell of him thin. . . . Crucifixion. Disembowelment. Fire. Gas in the shower room. . . . The pull of the rack. The suck of the sea. . . ." When he turns to Angela, asking her to put her arm around him for comfort, she awakens from her untroubled sleep only long enough to change positions; she fails to reach him.

Angela calmly accepts "the truth, we go into the ground and don't know anything and come back as grass." Thus Angela cannot understand Piet's fear and hatred of Freddy Thorne, for Freddy represents the decay that is not threatening to Angela but that Piet is mustering all his physical and spiritual resources to deny. Angela's calm acceptance of the natural cycle, her characterization as undersexed and untroubled, leaves Piet's spirit free, unsuffocated by the all-absorbing sensuality that Foxy represents to him. Thus Piet's acceptance of Foxy represents a capitulation, an abandonment of his spiritual search. Updike has said that Piet "divorces the supernatural to marry the natural." [4]

Angela is thus associated with Piet's spiritual potential throughout the novel. Her name is Angela, she comes from Nun's Bay, she has "a superior power seeking through her to employ him," being with her is "heaven." Responding to her lack of physicality, Piet thinks, "Touch Angela, she vanished." Her tone implies "a disdain of sex" and she is "above it all." When they make love it is "as if a visitor from space has usurped his wife's body." When his affair with Foxy is revealed, Piet pleads that Angela not dismiss him, telling her, "You're what guards my soul. I'll be damned eternally."

Foxy's contrasting physicality is also reinforced by

her name, which is often shortened to "Fox," an animal of prey. Her association with flowers throughout the
novel again connects her to the temporal and the sensual;
Piet imagines himself her "secret gardener." In contrast
to the naturalness and temporality of flowers, stars are immortal and untouchable; thus it is with stars that Angela
is associated throughout the novel.

After building up the association between Angela and
stars, Updike enlarges the implications of star references
in his description of Freddy Thorne's party the night of
John Kennedy's assassination. Dancing as if "on the pol-
ished top of Kennedy's casket," the couples play songs that
record the gradual disappearance of the stars, from "Stars
Fell on Alabama" through "Stardust" to "Under a Blan-
ket of Blue." When Piet leaves the dancing it is to leave
Angela as well, and to seek Foxy, whom he kneels before
in the bathroom, nursing from her lactating breasts.
When Angela knocks on the bathroom door he escapes
through the window. To a couple outside, his "fall" from
the second-story window seems from the sky. It is an in-
dividualized case of the fall of Adam.

Piet is aware that his abandonment of Angela for
Foxy is a fall, from the heavenly to the earthly, from stars
to flowers. He knows that flowers do not bloom forever,
that to accept Foxy and abandon himself totally to sexuality represents a spiritual death. Angela's lack of physicality does not suffocate his spirit; Foxy's demanding,
sensual hunger, her overwhelming desire to own all of
Piet, does smother the religious impulse. Updike has said
that at the end of *Couples* Piet "becomes a satisfied person
and in a sense dies." [5]

In two scenes early in the novel Updike predicts Piet's
ultimate fate. The first is a basketball game at which Piet
injures Freddy, as he does when he takes Georgene
Thorne as his mistress early in the novel. Freddy goes to
Angela, who splints his hurt finger, as she will later attempt to stiffen Freddy's other limp member. Piet

kneels to Freddy, mockingly asking forgiveness, as he will later submit to him, calling him a "savior," for arranging the abortion. Pretending his splinted finger is a death ray, Freddy points it at Piet, among others, saying, "Zizz. Die," thus foretelling Piet's spiritual death.

The story of his daughter's pet hamster also parallels Piet's fate. The hamster is male, with amber fur the color of Piet's hair, and the sound of its wheel in the cage at night is comforting to Piet, for he thinks the treadmill will get the hamster to Heaven. But when it escapes its cage, the hamster is killed by an animal of prey, in this case a cat. Piet buries it among the flowers, wondering as he does it why he feels moved by the death of something so small.

Unlike Piet, Foxy does not feel her adoration for her lover is an abandonment of Christianity, a kind of spiritual death. At the end of the novel she still considers herself a Christian, whereas Piet does not. There is, for her, a continuity and not a conflict between the natural and the supernatural. For her, fellating is equivalent to the Eucharist. For Piet oral sex is the adoration of the lover, but not God.

Piet's request that Freddy arrange the abortion of his child signifies his submission to Freddy, and to this world of death and decay. Not only does Piet kill the child, but in doing so he kills the residual faith that made him tell Freddy earlier, "I think you are professionally obsessed with decay. Things grow as well as rot." The abortion is an analogue of his spiritual death; he kills "a seed that bore his face." Piet tells Foxy that what he destroyed "wasn't a child, it was a little fish, less than a fish. It was nothing, Fox." But the fish is a symbol for Christ, and in assenting to the abortion, Piet has symbolically destroyed the last of his Christian faith. It is an action that binds Piet to death and to the natural world and makes him, in his own mind, a "murderer."

The serious sympathy that Updike shows Piet is a re-

flection of his high regard for the writings of Denis de
Rougemont. De Rougemont explains romantic love in contemporary Western culture by tracing it back to courtly
love, and from there to a neo-Manichaean heresy that
Updike, in a review of one of de Rougemont's works, describes this way:

Manichaenism, denying the Christian doctrines of the
Divine Creation and the Incarnation, radically opposes the
realms of spirit and matter. The material world is evil.
Man is imprisoned in the darkness of the flesh. His only
escape is through asceticism and mystical "knowing."
Women are Devil's lures designed to draw souls down into
bodies; on the other hand, each man aspires toward a
female Form of Light who is *his own true spirit*, resident in
Heaven, aloof from the Hell of matter.[6]

Couples is a statement of the impossibility of the individual female to become the male's spiritual ideal; the failure
of this, and the male's commitment nonetheless to the female, results in his abandonment of the search for *"his
own true spirit."*

   Critics have seen similarities between Piet Hanema
and two of de Rougemont's favorite lovers, both mentioned by Updike in this review.[7] First there is Don Juan,
the legendary lover whose promiscuous search was, presumably, for an impossible ideal. Second, and more convincingly, there is Tristan, the lover of Isolde, who, because she was married, became the Unattainable Lady,
Tristan's ideal woman. Regardless of whether Updike
created Piet as an echo of either or both of these figures,
certainly there is an intimate connection between his
opinions on de Rougemont and *Couples*. Updike might
have been describing Piet's dilemma when he says in the
review:

Our fundamental anxiety is that we do not exist—or will
cease to exist. Only in being loved do we find external
corroboration of the supremely high valuation each ego
secretly assigns itself.[8]

While Updike's portrait of Piet is serious and sympathetic, his characterization of Freddy Thorne and some of the minor characters in the novel is critical and satirical, reflecting the author's reservations about sex as the emergent religion. The characterization of Freddy Thorne is the most powerful and original in *Couples,* and with his portrait, Updike shows the excesses to which sexual obsession could lead contemporary American society. Freddy is the priest of the emergent religion; he directs the rituals, the games and parties; arranges affairs and abortions; and attempts to convert others to the cult. Freddy thinks the couples have "made a church of each other." The god of the new church is death and decay, while sex, which is always linked with mortality in Updike's fiction, brings the new god closer.

Sexual sacraments have replaced the old Christian ones. Freddy tells partygoers early in the novel what Piet will only discover at its end, when he becomes a bona fide member of the new church and enjoys oral sex with Foxy on Sunday morning: "To fuck is human, to be blown, divine." Using sacramental language, Freddy equates fornication with fasting and party snacks to the Eucharist.

Freddy believes "People are the only thing people have left since God packed up. By people I mean sex. Fucking." So we're trying to "break back into" hedonism, he tells the couples who are gathered at a ski lodge for a weekend. While the couples sometimes dissociate themselves from Freddy's outrageous remarks, he is simply admitting what they furtively practice. It is directly after this sermon at the ski lodge that the Applebys and Smiths acknowledge their mutual affairs by going to each other's spouse's bedroom. Later, planning fourplay in the Appleby's living room, they quote Freddy.

Freddy's priestly connections are made clear in his dental office, where decay is supreme and abortions are arranged. The office is a "sanctum" in which Freddy ap-

pears with palms "uplifted in surprise of blessing, in front
of his backwards white jacket" like the backwards collar
of a priest. It is in this office that Piet offers Freddy
money as a bribe for arranging the abortion. But Freddy
responds to Piet's bribe by saying, "Surely, old friend,
we have moved beyond money as a means of exchange"
and proposes a night with Angela as the sacrifice re-
quired of the sinner.

But the portrait of Freddy *is* satirical, in contrast to
the sympathetic portrayal of Piet. In spite of all his brave
pronouncements advocating sex, and arguing the omni-
presence of death and decay in this world, Freddy is still
attracted to the immaterial and the immortal, so much so
that he is impotent in the physical world. For, judged by
the standards of the religion he preaches, Freddy is a failure. His obsession with sex has emasculated him, to such
an extent that he is sometimes presented to us as androg-
ynous, other times as having homosexual tendencies.
Preaching sex, he practices it ineffectually; his wife finds
him an unsatisfactory lover, and he is impotent the evening that he spends with Angela.

When the couples play the game "Wonderful,"
Freddy tells them that "The most wonderful thing I know
is the human capacity for self-deception." The very basis
of satire is "the human capacity for self-deception" and,
although Freddy sees it all around him, he fails to per-
ceive it in himself. Although he preaches complete sensual
enjoyment of the physical world, he loves Angela for what
seems to him her lack of physicality. She is his "ideal," his
"saint." When he goes to bed with her, Freddy suffers a
disillusionment that reveals his self-deception to us,
though not to him. Angela's sexual willingness embar-
rasses him, her flesh dismays him. "That Angela, the
most aloof of women . . . should harbor in her clothes
the same voracious spread of flesh as other women af-
flicted Freddy . . . with the nausea of disillusion." The disillusionment causes Freddy to be impotent, and the scene

closes with his masturbating beside the sleeping Angela, "taking care not to defile her." Surely Updike is satirizing the high priest of hedonism here.

The human capacity for self-deception is also carefully revealed in the portrait of several minor characters, making them satirical. The conscious hypocrisy of these other couples is posed against the seriousness and conviction of Piet. For instance, Updike makes a point of telling us that the Applesmith's morality "proved to be merely consciousness of the other couples watching them." Updike emphasizes that all of their sexual alliances are based not only on a deception of each other, but also a self-deception which makes them satirical targets.

Let us look, for instance, at the scene in the ski lodge when Frank and Harold arrange to go to each other's wife's room. To appreciate this scene we have to realize the deception being practiced. Frank and Harold are having affairs with each other's wives. But while Harold knows about both his and Frank's affair, Frank does not know that his wife is being unfaithful. In this scene he thinks he is arranging a first encounter between his wife and Harold, an affair he wants to encourage in order to facilitate his own alliance with Harold's wife.

Still the two couples were slow to go upstairs. Freddy's sad lewdness had stirred them. . . . [Harold] said, as if on Frank's behalf, "Freddy is very sick. *Très malade*." . . . Again Frank cleared his throat, but said nothing.

Up the upstairs hall, with its row of sleeping doors, Harold felt his arm touched. He had been expecting it. Frank whispered, mortified and hoarse, "Do you think we have the right rooms?"

Harold quickly said, "We're in nine, you're in eleven."

"I mean, do you think you and I should switch?"

From the elevation of his superior knowledge, Harold was tempted to pity this clumsy man groveling in lust. Daintily he considered, and proposed: "Shouldn't the ladies be consulted? I doubt if they'll concur."

Of course Harold knows all along that the ladies *will* concur, have in fact been "concurring" for some time. But while Harold is having his fun with Frank, Updike is making satirical thrusts at them both. Is Harold's really a "superior knowledge" and is it only Frank who is "grovelling in lust"? Finally, is it just Freddy who is *très malade* (very sick)?

To this point I have concentrated on the characters of *Couples* in an attempt to demonstrate that they incorporate both a celebrative and a satirical purpose in the novel. Updike's portraits of Freddy and of the Applesmiths deliberately demonstrate the triviality of sexual obsession and point it out graphically. Yet Updike still insists that Piet is worthy of our deep concern; he admires or at least strongly sympathizes with Piet's move from supernaturalism to naturalism. There is then a certain creative tension in *Couples* between the apparent poles of judgment and sympathy, of satire and celebration. This creative tension has produced what are, in the novel, both satirical and celebrative sexual symbols.

The celebrative symbols in *Couples* are natural and evocative, reflecting traditional sexual imagery, such as in the references to flowers and the sea. The proximity of Foxy's house to the sea, her associations with both the sea and flowers, reinforce her sexuality. The flowers die after they blossom and thus reflect the inevitable mortality of the natural world. In this respect they are a link with Piet's dead parents, who owned greenhouses where the child Piet helped plant seeds and water blossoms, causing flowers to bloom.

While Angela's sexuality is compared to the shallow bath in which she washes herself of Piet, Foxy, making love, is a "Machine that makes salt at the bottom of the sea," an elemental force. The sea as sexual symbol gains richness in its extension to Freddy, who is often described in terms of a sea creature, and in one scene wears the wetsuit and fins of a diver. That his impotence should be the harvest of the sea, that as a fish he becomes the new Christ, is both subtly ironic and appropriate.

The most important sexual symbol in *Couples* is the weathercock that stands atop the steeple of the Congregational Church, and it is the cock alone that survives the fire that destroys the church. In the initial reviews of *Couples,* that rooster came in for a lot of criticism, a barrage of complaints more or less summed up in the accusation that it is "clumsily symbolic." [9] Other critics rose to the defense of the cock, elaborating the appropriateness of its penny eye, its variability in the wind, and its ritual function.[10] Yet these unsatisfactory interpretations are all based on an incomplete understanding of Updike's purpose, which is both celebrative and satirical even in the presentation of this symbol.

It is true that when the cock is first introduced it has a celebrative function. At the beginning of the novel it is "A golden rooster," "high above Tarbox," "a gilded weathercock" that "flashed in the sun and served as a landmark to fishermen." "Children in the town grew up with the sense that the bird was God." It is "unreachable."

But at the end of the novel the rooster is no longer unreachable; it has fallen. An enormous and elaborate mechanical erection rescues the cock from atop the gutted church. Moreover, in this last scene the children who thought the bird was God have become "jeering," the golden rooster has become "the piece of tin," and the gilt has become "dull metal" that the pastor poses with, for photographs.

This is the work of the satirical and not the celebrative artist. And so it should be. For all that the characters of the novel have conveyed to us about sex, both its positive and negative aspects, is also conveyed to us in the image of the cock; it *can* be golden, it *can* reach toward heaven, it *can*, at the same time, become trivial and dull if it becomes so easily accessible that even clergymen embrace it. It can become as mechanical as it does with the Applesmiths or as religious as it becomes with Piet and Foxy. The symbol is, like the novel, both celebrative and satirical.

6

Bech: A Book

The first story about Henry Bech that Updike wrote was "The Bulgarian Poetess," which was published in *The New Yorker* and received the O. Henry Award in 1966. This story, like several of the others in *Bech: A Book,* is partially based on Updike's experiences during a tour he took in 1964–65 to Russia, Rumania, Bulgaria, and Czechoslovakia as part of the U.S.S.R.-U.S. Cultural Exchange Program. After the success of this first story, Updike, "never wanting to let a good thing go unflogged," as he puts it, wrote another and then another story about Bech. It was not until he had done four of the final seven stories that Updike "began to think that they might be a book." Thus *Bech: A Book* "was indeed conceived piecemeal," [1] and Updike's refusal to call it a novel reveals his awareness of its episodic nature and tenuous unity.

The unity of the collection is achieved primarily through the consistently comic tone of the stories and their common protagonist. The comic mood is established in the first page of the preface, where Updike leads us to believe that Bech, a contemporary American Jewish writer, is a real historical personage. We are asked to believe that Henry Bech wrote the preface, after he had read the stories about himself written by John Updike. Thus the preface begins "Dear John," and continues, commending Updike on some of the stories, finding fault with

his presentation of Bech in others. He includes "a list of
suggested deletions, falsifications, suppressions, and re-
cordings," all of which, Updike tells us, "have been
scrupulously incorporated."

The sense of fun established here remains throughout the collection, indeed until the final pages, where we
find a fake Bibliography, first of books by Bech, and then
of "Critical Articles Concerning" Bech. These last are up-
roarious, for they are phony articles by real critics in real
magazines, satirically exposing the parasitic nature of
critics, who feed upon the artist as they destroy him. Thus
the list includes an article called "Bech's Mighty Botch"
by Marcus Klein, "Bech's Noble Novel" by Norman Podhoretz, and an *E-Z Outline* on Bech's best novel by the
critic Leslie Fiedler.

The character of Bech, gradually unfolding through
the seven stories, also unites the collection. While Bech's
character is comic, the humor is not without a tinge of
sadness. Henry Bech is the author of one good novel, his
first, which became the "post-Golding, pre-Tolkien fad of
college undergraduates." Ever since the phenomenal success of that first novel he has attempted to produce its
equal. He has failed and is, at the time of the stories, unable to write at all. His chief literary efforts of the last
five years are reviews and minor articles (like "My Favorite Books" for the *New York Times*). He has also
created a series of rubber stamps with which he answers
his mail (presumably to avoid writing). The stamps read:

HENRY BECH REGRETS THAT HE
DOES NOT SPEAK IN PUBLIC.

HENRY BECH IS TOO OLD AND ILL
AND DOUBTFUL TO SUBMIT TO
QUESTIONNAIRES AND INTERVIEWS.

IT'S YOUR PH.D. THESIS;
PLEASE WRITE IT YOURSELF.

In spite of the stamps, throughout the stories Bech finds himself increasingly involved in guest lectures, interviews, public ceremonies, and the like, in order to avoid the blank page in his typewriter. Although he fears travel, he accepts an invitation from the State Department as a cultural ambassador on a lecture tour of the Iron Curtain countries. In Russia he frantically spends rubles that he cannot export. In Rumania he is homesick at Hanukkah, terrified of his wildly careening chauffeur, and makes what the State Department calls "contact" with a Rumanian writer whom they view as "Red hot" and "inaccessible," but who takes Bech to a girlie show and exchanges no more than two words with him. In Bulgaria he meets a poetess whom he instinctively recognizes as his long-sought-after ideal woman. Their last meeting is at a crowded reception for him where he cannot penetrate the crowd to get to her, and they part, never to see each other again. Once home again, Bech evades his typewriter and his mistress by accepting an invitation to speak at a girl's school in Virginia and by going to England on a promotional tour to advertise the English edition of his earlier work.

Bech's impotence at the typewriter has spread to bed, but marriage-minded mistresses still attempt to lead him to the altar. But he fears marriage as he fears all new experiences, and his mistresses become embittered harpies who castigate him. "You are sick, Henry. You are weak, and sick," accuses one mistress, while another tells him "after keeping you company for three years I've forgotten what goes on in any normal man's mind."

The ironic humor of these stories is partly created by the repeated motif of missed opportunities, recognitions that come too late to Bech. For example, innocent of publisher's wiles, he sold the rights to his first, most successful novel at a shocking disadvantage so that, years later, he is impoverished while his publisher grows fat; the contracts on his later books are much more to his advantage, but the books do not sell. Another recognition that comes too late occurs at the airport as he is leaving Russia, where, kissing his guide good-bye, "he realized, horrified, that he should have slept with her." In other stories he realizes, too late, that the marijuana offered to him by an adoring student makes him terribly ill, and that a trip to Virginia to escape depression only leads to deeper despair.

Updike creates a similar humor with a pattern of disappointed expectations, the flip side of missed opportunities. Hoping for a favorable review, Bech slavishly submits to prolonged and boring interviews with the literary editor of the *London Observer;* he is rewarded with an article in the paper entitled "Bech's Best Not Good Enough." In Bulgaria Bech arranged for the lovely poetess to be invited to his final reception and he "looked forward to seeing her again." But at the party he is trapped by "a rasping American female" seeking advice for her adolescent nephew who wants to be a writer; thus Bech gets only a hurried exchange with his ideal woman. Even being rich is disappointing, for the money, given in rubles for Russian translations of his work, cannot be exported from Russia and must be squandered on cheap merchandise and frivolous furs for mistresses past and present. Most important, the final story, "Bech in Heaven," presents the disappointment suffered by Bech when he realizes that art does not guarantee immortality.

But the quality that creates sympathy for the protagonist who is subject to these constant regrets and disappointments is his self-knowledge. Henry Bech knows that "his reputation had grown while his powers declined," and the knowledge is painful to him. In the story "Bech Panics," he feels a "devastating sadness. . . . He knew that he was going to die. That his best work was behind him." This recognition leads to what Updike describes as "a 'religious crisis' that, by all standard psychology, should have been digested in early adolescence, along with post-masturbatory guilt." Ashamed of the emotional maelstrom he is in, yet desperate, believing that he has achieved nothing in his life, Bech finally flings himself on the damp earth, begging and praying for mercy from "Someone, Something." But he succeeds only in being bitten by insects and getting his pant knees dirty.

The comic tone of *Bech: A Book* is partly created by the complete absence of the supernatural. A scene such as the one described above is comically anticlimactic only when we have been subtly assured all along that Bech expects no answer to his prayers. Indeed, except in this one scene, *Bech* makes no reference to the supernatural world. Instead, Bech's religion is his art. It is through his writing that he hopes to achieve the immortality that most of us seek through religion.

But for Updike, the substitution of art for religion, the adoration of the word rather than the Word, has always been a futile and faintly ridiculously pursuit. Updike has written, "No aesthetic theory will cover the case," [2] and his reviews reflect his reservations about treating art as an end in itself, as a substitute religion.

The futility of Bech's hope for literary immortality is obvious from the first. He cannot write; his most popular book is described as a "fad," his most ambitious work is a "flop." The very words "fad" and "flop" emphasize the transience of Bech's appeal. But the failure of Bech's expectations are most movingly, and comically, expressed in the final story of the volume, "Bech Enters Heaven."

The story begins as a flashback to when Henry's mother took the young boy of thirteen not to his bar mitzvah but to a ceremony in which the American cultural greats of that period were honored. Breathless and star-struck in the balcony of a massive, domed Greek-revival auditorium, the boy Bech idolized these immortals who had transcended time through their art; "they had attained the haven of lasting accomplishment and ex-

empted themselves from the nagging nuisance of growth
and its twin—decay."

Many years later, as a middle-aged novelist, Bech
"received, in an envelope not so unlike those containing
solicitations to join the Erotica Book Club or the Associated Friends of Apache Education, notice of his election
to a society whose title suggested that of a merged
church, with an invitation to its May ceremonial." He
accepts "because in his fallow middle years he hesitated
to decline any invitation," not realizing that the society
he has been invited to join is the "Pantheon" of cultural
greats that he idolized as a boy. When he arrives at the
ceremony it is not until he is escorted onto the stage
that he realizes he has become one of the immortals.
"He was here. He had joined that luminous, immutable
tableau. He had crossed to the other side."

But as he looks around him, he sees fellow artists in
various stages of decay and dissipation. They are blind,
or semiparalytic, or grotesquely bent, or deaf. Some of
them are stoned (on drugs or alcohol), others sleep
through the ceremony, others are so senile they rock,
mumbling, in their chairs. He is told by an aging writer,
partly deaf, with dyed hair, false teeth, and sour breath,
the circumstances of his election to the honored company: "Jesus Christ, Bech, I've been plugging for you for
years up here, but the bastards always said, 'Let's wait
until he writes another book, that last one was such a
flop.' Finally I say to them, 'Look. The son of a bitch,
he's *never* going to write another book,' so they say 'O.K.,
let's let him the hell in.' Welcome aboard, Bech."

Updike has told us that Bech "wants to be lifted out
of the flux the way literary immortals are," [3] but in this
story he is again bitterly disappointed, realizing that "literary immortals" are merely mortals, that what he had
imagined as heaven is "a cardboard tableau lent sub-
stance only by the credulous." But, in spite of this recognition, Bech goes through the ceremonial welcoming of

new members, stands for the insincere introduction in which his name is mispronounced, submits to the handshake and the applause.

It is this willingness of Bech to succumb to the demands of the society in which he lives that distinguishes him from Updike's more serious protagonists. All the Bech stories create a comic view of the victimization of its main character and a coinciding reduction in his importance reflected by authorial distance from him. While Updike's serious protagonists may also be viewed as victims, they are victims of an inner drive, a sense of mission that leads them to defy the dictates of society. Bech never defies society.

In his comic subservience to the demands of society "Bech becomes a showman against his will. A display piece. A toy." [4] He submits to being used by women, by colleges and students, and by the State Department, which wants him for propaganda purposes. All the while he regrets what he has missed and hopes for more than he gets.

7

Rabbit Redux

A successful sequel is a rarity in fiction, yet Updike achieved this exceptional accomplishment with the publication of *Rabbit Redux* in 1971. Reviewers were almost unanimous in their praise of the novel, and overwhelmingly generous with superlatives. Indeed, it could be argued that *Rabbit Redux* is Updike's greatest imaginative achievement, for it is written without reference to the Christian or classical myths upon which his earlier novels depended. Rabbit reflects this secularization in his lack of spiritual drive and his consequent loss of that tension between the spiritual and the carnal that most of Updike's protagonists struggle with. The only thing that this Rabbit believes in is his country, and this novel is an intense examination of that American dream in light of the events of the sixties.

In Book 1 of *Rabbit Redux* we are introduced to a middle-aged, conservative, conventional, spiritually and sexually diminished Rabbit Angstrom. Having returned to his wife and child ten years earlier, Rabbit has dedicated himself to American ideals, fulfilling his duty to family and flag. He has been faithfully working as a linotypist at the printing company where his father is employed, and he has bought a home in the suburbs. As the novel opens Rabbit's father reports to him rumors that Janice is having an affair with one of the salesmen at her father's used-car lot where she now works. Over the next few days Rabbit's suspicions become certainties, and he confronts Janice; she admits to the affair and, faced with Rabbit's indifference, leaves him for her lover. Rabbit remains to take care of their son, Nelson, now thirteen. In the final scene of Book 1, father and son visit Rabbit's mother, who is slowly dying of Parkinson's disease.

In Book 2 a black worker at the printing company where Rabbit is employed invites him to a bar where he meets Jill, a white, eighteen-year-old runaway from a rich but uncaring family. Jill goes home with Rabbit and they make love, although Jill's total lack of self-concern makes Rabbit sad and sexually passive. When Nelson meets Jill the next morning they immediately like each other, and throughout the novel their relationship is like that of close siblings. The three of them live fairly peacefully for several weeks, punctuated by Janice's jealous phone calls and the sadly desperate lovemaking of Jill and Rabbit, who seem equally lost.

But in Book 3 this relative calm is disrupted by the arrival of Skeeter, a young black Vietnam veteran, now a revolutionary, whom Jill knew before she met Rabbit. Skeeter has jumped bail for drug possession, and he and Jill ask Rabbit to let him stay for a few nights. Rabbit reluctantly consents, but there is constant tension between the patriotic middle-class white man and the militant black. As the days stretch into weeks, Jill and Nelson arrange for nightly discussions to open up communication. Smoking grass with the others, Rabbit learns about Afro-American history, Vietnam, the treatment of blacks by the law, and the corruption of a system based on exploitation. Jill becomes increasingly and unwillingly dominated by Skeeter, who now has her hooked on hard drugs. Eventually both Skeeter and Rabbit share Jill sexually while she, almost unaware, in a drug-induced daze, passively complies.

Neighborhood delegates, whose children have been

spying on these sexual activities, complain to Rabbit and
threaten him: they want the black man out of their white
neighborhood. Meantime Rabbit has been receiving and
declining repeated invitations from the divorced mother
of one of Nelson's friends. Finally, when Nelson goes to
spend the night with his friend, Rabbit goes to spend the
night with the friend's mother, leaving Jill and Skeeter
alone in his house. Alerted by a call at 1 a.m., Rabbit
returns to find his house ablaze, Jill burned to death,
and Skeeter missing. The police, convinced that Skeeter
set the fire, put out a warrant for him. When Skeeter
tells him neighbors started the fire, Rabbit helps him
escape the city, on the understanding that he never
return.

Book 4 begins with Rabbit's dismissal from his job,
where he has been made redundant by new mechanized
printing techniques. We learn that after the fire Rabbit
and Nelson moved into Rabbit's parents' house. After
several weeks, Rabbit's sister, Mim, arrives home for a
visit. She is a Las Vegas call girl, attractive, thoroughly
realistic, totally in control. She amuses and delights them
all, coaxing Nelson out of his withdrawal and grief over
Jill, temporarily reviving her dying mother, and talking
Rabbit out of the depression and self-pity that he, home-
less, jobless, wifeless, and feeling guilt over Jill's death,
has fallen into.

Before she leaves, Mim arranges to meet Janice's
lover and has an affair with him. Janice leaves her lover
and, a few days later, phones Rabbit. They meet and, at
her invitation, go to a motel, where she and Rabbit fall
asleep in each other's arms.

All the events of the novel occur against an omni-
present background of the specific historical events of the
summer and fall of 1969. Rabbit watches SDS demonstrations, black riots in the inner cities, interviews with
black revolutionaries, fighting in Vietnam, and the popular shows of the sixties, like "Laugh-In," nightly on his

television. Rabbit hears about Chappaquiddick, goes to
see the movie *2001,* and has a "Lunar Special" at
Burger Bliss. Moreover, many of the conversations in the
novel revolve around current events, particularly the
United States involvement in Vietnam, which Rabbit
thoroughly supports.

But the most consistent historical references throughout the novel are to the moon landing in July 1969. The
prefix to each of the four sections of the novel are fragments taken from recorded conversations of the astronauts. Rabbit watches both the Apollo takeoff and the
moon landing on television. Moreover, Updike suffuses
the novel with space-age terminology, even in reference to
the everyday actions of the characters, so that the emptiness of outer space informs their very lives. For example,
at the end of the novel, when Rabbit is in bed with
Janice, he is described as "adjusting in space, slowly
twirling . . . drifting along sideways," with her, and
after Janice "rotates" her body, Rabbit drifts into sleep
with a floating sensation. All the characters except Skeeter
are pale and almost ghostly, often dressed in grey or dirty
white, associating them with the TV images of the astronauts. The city and its suburbs are a bleak and barren
terrain, having a "desolate openness" so deserted that, at
one point, Rabbit questions: "Is there life on Earth?"
The empty wasteland of the city, where man is utterly
alone and almost alien, is thus made analogous to the
moon.

The intricate interplay of the space allusions combine to reinforce the complete absence of the supernatural in *Rabbit Redux.* Through his technological skill
man has succeeded in penetrating the heavens that sur-
round him. But he has found them empty, and the moon,
a traditional mythical symbol, is "a big round nothing."
The emptiness of outer space is reflected by the emptiness
within Rabbit, an internal void where his spirit and his
emotional attachments to others once lived. When, at the

end of the novel, Janice asks Rabbit, "Who do you think you are?" he answers truthfully, "Nobody."

But the events of the sixties are not only the background for the novel; they provide the basis for its action. Given the exclusion of the supernatural in *Rabbit Redux*, Updike expands his art horizontally rather than vertically, making the individual event representative of national history and making particular characters representative of whole classes. In this way Updike expands the implications of *Rabbit Redux* so that the novel becomes a paradigm of contemporary American history, a representation of the general sociopolitical movements of the sixties. The major characters become representative without losing their credibility as individuals, and the situations remain convincing, while they reflect the historical event.

Updike demonstrates this representative purpose in his description of Rabbit's suburban tract house, a house that is duplicated all over America and that becomes, in the novel, a microcosm of America, containing all its diverse factions. Its synthetic, assembly-line furnishings, its standardized appearance, like all the other houses on the street with their rows of television aerials pointing toward an empty sky, its picture window looking out over vacant lawns, all these details give the house an aura of anonymity. Just as television has become a focal point of American family life, so does Rabbit's set dominate the living room, always on. Once Jill and Skeeter arrive, however, they take the place of the national events that the nightly news portrays, and the TV becomes unnecessary. The historical event then becomes personal experience for Rabbit.

Updike's characterization of Rabbit encourages the reader to accept him as the representative white, middle-class American. He is a kind of American "everyman," [1] caught in the midst of events over which he has no control. Janice and her lover agree that Rabbit is the "silent majority" and "a normal product . . . a typical good-hearted imperialist racist." Skeeter repeatedly identifies him as "the Man." Even Nelson calls Rabbit "average and ordinary."

But at no time in his portrait of Rabbit does Updike sacrifice realistic for symbolic action. The individual peculiarities of Rabbit's character are too clearly delineated to make him seem only a stereotype. We are willing to accept, on a realistic level, the changes that have occurred in the ten years since *Rabbit, Run,* slight modifications that lead us to think of Rabbit as less exceptional, more "common," and thus more fit for his role as the representative blue-collar worker living in suburbia, clinging to his conservative beliefs and faith in America.

This patriotic faith has replaced Rabbit's earlier spiritual drive. He defends his country's actions in Vietnam, believing that America's ultimate purpose there is to "make a happy rich country, full of highways and gas stations." He identifies with the flag, so that in one argument the "treachery and ingratitude befouling the flag" is at the same time "befouling him." He has put a flag decal on his car. He supports the establishment on every issue, from Indian massacres of long ago to the race riots of today, and he is suspicious of hippies, demonstrators, blacks, and all those who criticize his country. At the opening of the novel he deplores the "Negroes plus the rich kids who want to pull it all down."

While Rabbit has accepted the conservative standards of society as they were urged upon him ten years before, many segments within that society have changed, ironically leaving him still out of step. Janice describes Rabbit's dilemma:

"Maybe he came back to me, to Nelson and me, for the old-fashioned reasons, and wants to live an old-fashioned life, but nobody does that any more, and he feels it. He put his life into rules he feels melting away now."

Janice herself demonstrates the relaxation of those "old-fashioned" rules. Her taking a job, having an affair, and finally leaving her home are representative of the growing liberation of women in the sixties. Yet in achieving this representative significance Updike has sacrificed none of Janice's credibility as a character, and the circumstances of her affair are convincingly detailed. Though freedom from Janice was what the earlier Rabbit had sought, now her departure releases him into space that he knows is empty. For Rabbit now "growth is betrayal," and as we get older, "we get emptier."

Rabbit's earlier spiritual drive is gone. At best his prayers have been sporadic and his Christianity is reduced to a few "Sunday school images." When Jill asks for a Bible to swear on, he says, "We've kind of let all that go." Part of the reason for Rabbit's rejection of religion lies in his personal past, in which his religious quest led to the death of his daughter. So now, for him, "Freedom means murder. Rebirth means death." This conviction leads to Rabbit's emotional emptiness; afraid of feeling and the suffering it may lead to, he consciously wills himself against caring for anyone except Nelson and his mother. Even Janice is ultimately expendable, for Rabbit's feelings are repeatedly described as frozen, as if he were on the cold and bleak terrain of the moon. He does not even care for himself and classifies himself as "about C minus" as a human being.

This emotional emptiness makes Rabbit a passive observer through most of the novel, while all the other characters conduct their private search for the answer. As Rabbit tells Jill, "I once took that inner light trip and all I did was bruise my surroundings." Yet even his lack of action produces feelings of guilt for Rabbit. When tragedy does occur, his passivity, his unwillingness to fight for Janice, his refusal to dismiss Skeeter from the house, his lack of concern for Jill, make him feel guilty in retrospect. Updike thus implies that the "silent majority" did indeed remain silent and passive through the sixties and, in so doing, somehow contributed to the chaos in this country.

At least part of the turmoil of the sixties was reflected by the white, predominantly upper middle class radicals who crowded the campuses, led demonstrations, and formed new drug cults in many urban centers, rejecting their families and the materialism they practiced. This group is represented in *Rabbit Redux* by Jill, who comes from a moneyed family but has rejected the American "system"; "I ran away from it," she says, "I reject it, I *shit* on it." She has dismissed both the "old God" and the "angry old patriotism" to which Rabbit and the society around him are dedicated, and she substitutes a vague new God perceived through the illumination (or hallucination) of drugs.

Jill believes in the negation of the individual ego and its selfish physical and material appetites. She scorns the material world, as we see in her neglect of the Porsche that was a gift from her parents. She tries to "rise above" the appetites that the ego asserts. Drugs facilitate this obliteration of the ego and open her mind, at first, to some vague apprehension beyond the reality of this world. But she doesn't realize that the destruction of the ego and its selfish appetites finally implies death.

Skeeter skillfully uses both Jill's anti-materialism and Rabbit's conservatism for his own selfish goals. We see him manipulating Rabbit when they first meet and Rabbit refuses to let him stay at the house. Rabbit's initial response to Skeeter is one of mixed fear and distrust; blacks were acceptable as long as they stayed at the back of the bus and kept quiet, fitting into the established order of the past. Skeeter, perceiving Rabbit's hostility, realizes that it is only by bringing it out in the open that they will have any basis for communication at all. So he goads Rabbit into a fight by insulting his American ideals from motherhood to the church, finally making Rabbit hit him in anger. When contact, even violent contact, is established, and when Rabbit shows his superior strength, he feels confident enough, and guilty enough, to allow the black to stay on in the house. Skeeter calls it "a little tokenism to wash your sins away."

Skeeter's role as representative of the black militant movement of the sixties involves the rejection of all things white, particularly the white man's hypocritical religion. Instead there will be a new religion, in which blackness will be worshipped. Because revolutionary blacks have this religious vision, an inner drive that Rabbit lacks, they have "soul." The whites in the novel have no soul; they lack religious vision, they know that beyond this world there is nothing but empty space.

Although it employs much of the terminology and ritual associated with the church, Skeeter's religion is as opposed to traditional white Christianity as black is to white. As an individual, he reflects the general rejection of Christianity among black militants in the sixties. Many of the black militants during that decade recognized that they had been cheated of their birthright by being promised immaterial rewards in heaven if they turned the other cheek in this world. They shifted their support instead to a new "religion" of black power (away from Martin Luther King to "Rap" Brown and Stokely Carmichael) that seeks to create a heaven on earth that would reward blacks with the material benefits they have long been denied.

The white Christianity that Skeeter wishes Rabbit to reject and the white man's belief in the American dream are inextricably linked; for Rabbit, the Good Samaritan and the Statue of Liberty are one and the same. So before preaching his new religion Skeeter must debunk the fantasy that white America has believed in, the American dream. "It was a *dream*," he tells Rabbit, "it was a state of mind from those poor fool pilgrims on." But it is a dream that Rabbit patriotically accepts, as

Skeeter himself realizes: "you say America to you and you still get bugles and stars but say it to any black or yellow man and you get hate, right?" Skeeter and Jill attempt to convince Rabbit that the white industrial worker in this "dollar-crazy" democracy is as much enslaved, economically, as the blacks.

Skeeter's goal coincides with Jill's insofar as they both reject the status quo. But Jill's purpose ends with destruction; her concern is not the redistribution but the rejection of material goods. In contrast, Skeeter knows the power that goes with material possessions and wants blacks to be the new elite. He sees the destruction of the system as an inevitable step toward this change. "That'll come anyway," he tells Rabbit, Jill, and Nelson, "That big boom. It's not the poor blacks setting the bombs, it's the offspring of the white rich. It's not injustice pounding at the door, it's impatience. . . . We must look past that, past the violence into the next stage."

According to Skeeter, Vietnam is the catalyst that will bring about the revolution and usher in a new era. It is the necessary turmoil that precedes redemption. Skeeter explains Rabbit's fascination for and approval of the war as the attraction that the common American, impotent in his own country, feels for a milieu in which he is able to express his anger and frustration, where he can feel like part of a power play. For the black man Vietnam is more than that, because in the equality that death deals out ("black body can stop a bullet as well as any other"), racial divisions disappear. In fact, Skeeter says, "I had white boys die for me," and it is this sacrificial death, so that he might live, that he wishes to extend to this country.

While all of these characters are individuals in their own right, they are also representative of larger social forces, active in America in the sixties. What I have been describing, with Jill and Skeeter, is the temporary alliance of the rich white radical youth with the black militant to overthrow the "System." If we are to equate this to events in the sixties, we must think of the student revolts, the predominantly white, upper-class youth who led the SDS, and the conviction, among black militants, that this disruption within the white majority could only benefit the black revolution. Stimulated by drugs and sexually liberated, the young white radical (Jill) and the black militant (Skeeter) live off the productiveness of the working class (Rabbit), attempting to change his conservatism while being sustained by his labor. They urge him to endorse the overthrow of the "System."

The farseeing black militant sees beyond this disintegration of the structure of American society to the building of a new order in which blacks provide the values and criteria. In this process, the blacks find the rich white radicals, indeed any whites, as expendable as they themselves were expendable for whites throughout American history. If the conservative white element can be used by "reeducating" him to the black militant's viewpoint, well and good. But if the education proves to have only minimal effect on the beliefs of the middle class, then the suburban society, and what it represents, contains the seeds of its own destruction. Its destruction lies in its unwillingness to change, to relinquish past values and ideals. Thus Rabbit's neighbors set fire to a house that is, in almost all respects, identical to their own, inadvertently killing, not the black, but the rich white radical youth. Or, Updike leaves us with the slight possibility that the black militant himself set fire to the house, destroying the suburban stronghold, killing the young white radical.

Rabbit's submission to Skeeter is not unconditional even when it is most strongly felt. Although he occasionally says "I believe," he will also on occasion tell Skeeter that his rage is the result of "pure self-pity," or that the readings from black history are "bleeding heart stuff." Skeeter does make Rabbit aware of his formerly buried hatred of the rich professionals and industrialists, the exploiters of lower middle class whites as well as minorities. For example, Rabbit bitterly realizes his mother's dying "was a game being played by doctors who drove Caddies. . . ." Rabbit's opinions concerning American involvement in Vietnam are slightly altered as well so that, although he does not condemn it at the end of the novel, he no longer avidly defends it. As one reviewer writes: "Rabbit is deeply shaken by the extended encounter with Skeeter, literally and figuratively burned by it, but he plausibly remains more or less what he was." [2]

The fact that Rabbit and the way of life he represents are affected but not entirely destroyed by the events of the sixties is symbolized by the fire; this idea is developed in the last section of the novel. Although Jill dies in the fire and the bedroom, with its sexual connotations, is destroyed, Rabbit and his son are unharmed and the living room and Nelson's room are left almost intact. But the burning of the house marks a partial destruction of those ideals Rabbit held and which the middle-class suburban home represented. Nor do the implications of the fire stop with the middle-class suburb. Penn Park, the rich suburb that Rabbit's subdivision seeks to emulate, is also caught up in the destruction. Jill's death is the death of a Penn Park offspring, and the route to the fire is through the wealthy suburb, along *Ember*ly Avenue. All classes in white America are affected by this fire.

Because the fire symbolizes the destruction of a way of life that Updike has associated with the emptiness of space and the chaos in Vietnam, his description of it incorporates images connected with these events. This concentration on similarities between the moon, the war, and the burning of the suburban home makes the reader equate the three as mutually destructive to the American tradition. The lawn around the home becomes, like the astronauts' description of the lunar surface, "powdered charcoal." In his description of the war, Skeeter remembers victims of napalm "burning like a torch," as Jill must have done, her body so badly burned there is "no telling" whether she was black or white. Finally, the "green rubber bag" in which her body is removed is the same as those "shiny green body bags" that Skeeter remembers in Vietnam.

The deal that Rabbit makes, as he helps Skeeter escape, is that the black militant should never return. "I shall return," Skeeter promises, "only in glory," and with that thought Updike moves into the unforeseeable future. The scene in which Rabbit takes his leave of Skeeter is one full of ambiguous religious hints on a road marked Galilee 2.

So it was at the end of the sixties that the major spokesmen for the black movement withdrew from the national scene. By 1970 Malcolm X and Martin Luther King were assassinated, Rap Brown was arrested and imprisoned, and Stokely Carmichael and Eldridge Cleaver had fled to Africa. I am not suggesting that Skeeter represents any one of these, but rather that his individual portrait reflects the general historical withdrawal from aggressive action. When Rabbit leaves Skeeter it is a standoff of sorts, and only history will write the outcome.

If all this is a microcosm of the social and political unheavals of the sixties, what happens in Book 4 of the novel? Updike, uncannily attuned to the mood of the country, almost seems to be able to envisage the retrenchment of the seventies in that final section. In Book 4 of *Rabbit Redux* Updike portrays Rabbit's return to the past, where he finds a relative stability. Rabbit's return to his childhood home marks a return to his childhood habits. He finds in himself "an appetite for boyish foods"; he plays basketball and wears his high school clothes; and he masturbates in his boyhood bed.

In this environment love is renewed. Rabbit finally finds within himself grief for Jill and recognizes his former hardness toward her as part of the "deadness" into which he had retreated. This last section, then, reasserts the value of human love, its power to sustain life, if not to defeat death. Rabbit's return is, his mother claims, "worth a hundred doses" of the medicine she takes, and her slow death is temporarily delayed by human love.

Mim dominates the last section of the novel. She is someone who has adjusted to the emptiness of the contemporary world, learning to live in it as she has learned to live in the desert. Instead of looking for divine law, she lives by self-imposed rules for survival: "They're survival rules, rules for living in the desert," she tells Rabbit. Thus for her there is none of Rabbit's residual Christianity or love of country.

Rabbit's mother offers him similar rules for survival. She tells him, "Inch by inch. . . . Life is a cinch. Yard by yard, life is hard." As he sits beside his dying mother, Rabbit absorbs this advice. He recognizes the inevitability of mutability and death, and the necessity of maintaining a short-range view, because the long-range questions must go unanswered. "Time is our element, not a mistaken invader," he realizes, and this realization implies that, in the future, change may be a little less painful for him.

Rabbit's return to Janice is also a return to the past. He has accepted empty space as their milieu, and his reunion with Janice becomes an adjustment in space to another person's being close. The motel they go to may indeed turn out to be a "Safe Haven" as it is named, but Updike's final words are an enigmatic question: "He. She. Sleeps. O.K.?"

Is Rabbit's return to the past in this last section of the novel regressive? Or is Updike telling us that to go forward we must go back? Certainly Updike is fulfilling the representative purpose of the novel in this final section as well as the first three. In describing a wistful retreat

into the past, we can see reflected the popularity, in the
seventies, of nostalgic films, old-fashioned clothing styles,
handicrafts, and natural foods. Moreover, like Rabbit,
the middle class early in the seventies seemed to regain
its equilibrium as the violence of the sixties dissipated.
The "silent majority," reeling from a decade of destruction and disorder, retreated to what seemed to be a
reaffirmation of family life and democratic ideals.

To interpret the events and the characters of *Rabbit
Redux* as both individual and representative is not to
reduce it simply to an allegory of American sociopolitical
events. The characters are delineated in such detail, and
the circumstances of the plot are so convincingly created,
that realism is not sacrificed to the general historical
import of the novel. While they remain convincing individuals, Updike's characters become the agents of
history.

8

A Month of Sundays

I have always felt that *A Month of Sundays* is the most underrated of Updike's novels. Published in 1974, the novel drew unenthusiastic reviews and has generally been ignored since.[1] Critics overlooked the fact that beneath the fine sense of fun in the novel there is depth of characterization and an integration of thematic concerns that is new to Updike's fiction.

A Month of Sundays represents a breakthrough in its treatment of the dilemma of human duality that Updike has struggled with throughout his career. Until he wrote this novel, the body and the spirit, the ethical demands of this world and the desire to transcend the natural world, constantly opposed each other in Updike's fiction. Yet in *A Month of Sundays* Updike reaches a temporary but nonetheless balanced harmony of these formerly conflicting demands.

A Month of Sundays is the diary of Rev. Tom Marshfield, a New England minister who has been sent to a recuperation center for errant clergymen in a desert in the Southwest. Marshfield's offence involved the bedding of several married ladies in his congregation, though he assures us that rumor has exaggerated the actual number. His therapy for the month involves daily writing. In these daily diary entries that compose the novel itself, Marshfield recounts the events that led to this

temporary dismissal, interrupting his narrative each Sunday with a sermon.

Through the diary entries we learn about Marshfield's marriage twenty years earlier to the former Jane
Chillingworth, daughter of his ethics professor at semi-
nary. Like her father, Jane concentrates on ethical action
rather than spiritual fulfillment. Marshfield criticizes what
he feels is his wife's excessive social concern, saying,
"Jane doesn't believe in God, she believes in the Right
Thing."

In contrast, Tom Marshfield rejects this world and
its physical and social manifestations, desperately attempting to transcend the natural in search of the supernatural.
He writes, "What interests us is not the good but the
godly. Not living well, but living forever." Among the
aspects of the natural world that he repudiates are the
bulk of mankind, his own "rank" body and its hungers.
For Marshfield the body is "a swamp" in which the spirit
drowns.

But Marshfield's body, especially its sexual hungers,
will not be so easily dismissed. He is "as ready to stand
and ejaculate as to stand and spout the Apostles' Creed."
Among her good works Jane includes the sexual acquies-
cence of a dutiful wife. But Marshfield describes their
relations as "a marriage bed of nighttime solemnity and
spilt religion, spilt usually at the wrong angle, at the
moment when the cup has been withdrawn." His religious
metaphors indicate that Marshfield wants sex to be holy,
but the actual realization of this belief that the body is
sacred, that sex is "the exterior sign of interior grace,"
eludes him.

Marshfield's affair with Alicia Crick partially over-
comes his hatred and suspicion of his body and its appetites. Alicia is Marshfield's organist, whose expertise with
the male organ is equally instrumental. She "thinks with
her cunt" and teaches Marshfield "what fun" his "forgotten old body" could be. In bed she is for him "a

revelation" that supplants religious revelation. During their affair he finds it impossible to pray. Immersed in the natural, he rejects the supernatural. Representing abandonment to the completely physical, Alicia eventually urges Marshfield to leave both Jane and the ministry, both ethics and faith.

When Alicia confronts Jane with the affair, insisting that Marshfield must choose between them, he quickly drops Alicia and, for a brief period, returns to the "Right Thing," faithfulness to Jane. During this period Marshfield draws closer to his bearded and hip assistant minister, Ned Bork, who also devotes his life to doing good. Bork is always busy, holding benefits for Vietnamese refugees, arranging for adoptions, ministering to young drug addicts, or organizing volleyball for "the church oddballs," all the while wearing a sweat shirt emblazoned "Jesus Christ Superstar."

But Marshfield cannot accept this submergence in ethical action; he feels it suffocates the spiritual drive, the yearning for transcendence. The diary entries in which Marshfield describes this period of closeness to Bork and fidelity to Jane are followed by a Sunday sermon on Christ's miracles. Here Marshfield maintains that Christ's purpose was not to do good works to improve this world but to demonstrate, by a few selective miracles, the existence of a better world, a supernatural world. At the end of the sermon he seeks "a single mustard seed of faith," but he cannot find it.

Marshfield's search for faith, his desire to escape the solely ethical, leads to a liaison with Frankie Harlow, one of his parishioners. For Marshfield, Frankie does "embody faith." "Unlike Jane and Alicia, she was a believer." She is fragile, and fair, and unhappily married. But Marshfield cannot physically consummate their relationship. The act would desecrate the faith she represents; Marshfield is still unable to think of his body as holy, he is still unable to join body and spirit. His stubborn dicho-

tomy is revealed as he tells us, "I would greet my impotence as the survivor within me of faith, a piece of
purity amid all this relativistic concupiscence."

Physical consummation would be possible with Mrs.
Harlow, Marshfield realizes, only if she denies her faith.
So he subjects her to a litany of denial: " 'You dumb
cunt,' I said, 'how can you be so dumb as to believe in
God the Father, God the Son, and God the Holy Ghost?
Tell me you really don't. Tell me so I can fuck you.' "
But Mrs. Harlow holds steadfast to her faith, and Marsh-
field does not possess her.

Marshfield's education is, at the same time, being
continued by a group of women who seek their pastor's
ministrations for problems most often marital and sexual.
In his relations with these women Marshfield writes that
"an American mystery was circumscribed, having to do
with knowing, with acceptance of body by soul. . . ." In
his affairs with them he realizes they have achieved a
unity of body and spirit that still evades him:

They came to church the next Sunday with clean faces
and listened to the Word intent. There was a continuum for
them, where I felt a horrific gap. Bless them all. They
brought me out of the wilderness where I did not know
that our acts, every one, are homage.

Marshfield and Bork decide to dismiss Alicia as
organist because she, having had an affair with both, is
becoming an embarrassment. But she, vengeful, reveals
Marshfield's affairs to Frankie Harlow's husband, a church
deacon, who in turn reports to the bishop. Marshfield is
thus temporarily banished to the desert retreat for a
month from which, they assume, he will return penitent.

As Marshfield recounts the events summarized above,
he also includes occasional references in his diary to the
desert retreat in which he writes. It is managed by Ms.
Prynne, who, Marshfield suspects, reads his diary entries
as he writes them. Thus he occasionally stops his narrative

to address her, at first insultingly, as "prying Prynne," a threat to his privacy. As the diary continues he attempts to trap her into revealing her secret reading of his entries, with paper clips or hairs strategically placed on the page. She escapes these traps, and as Marshfield's entries begin to deal less with the past, more with the present, her influence on him is gradually revealed.

Marshfield has finished recounting his story by the third Sunday, and the sermon he writes that day reflects not only the therapeutic value of the writing he has done but also a new appreciation of the physical world, derived from Ms. Prynne's field trips. Ms. Prynne takes the clergymen on desert tours, during which Marshfield begins to recognize the richness of the desert that at first seemed empty and meaningless. He realizes the desert that surrounds him should be known not as Death Valley but by its Spanish name, La Palma de la Manos de Dios, the palm of God's hand.

Indeed, Marshfield goes on to identify much of the contemporary world—its pavements and parking lots, its bleak suburbs, even the lunar surfaces—as desert. He realizes this world, which once seemed to Marshfield an empty wilderness, a threat to his uncertain faith, is "to the acclimated vision," full of beauty. "And do we not see around us (with the knowledgeable guidance of our dear Ms. Prynne), the Joshua tree lifting its arms awkwardly in prayer, and hear the organ-pipe cactus thundering its transcendent hymn?" He hears "a chorale of praise" from the "invisible teeming of desert life," and he ends his third sermon appreciating this world rather than wishing to be out of it.

Ms. Prynne brings Marshfield to a new appreciation of not only the natural environment but also of the people who inhabit it. Her sympathetic treatment of a confused and drunken Indian during the clergymen's last field trip is an example of kindness and concern by which Marshfield learns a new definition of love. Instead of scorning or avoiding the Indian, Ms. Prynne listens to his mumbling, answers him, and with a delicacy born of sympathetic understanding, prevents him from making a spectacle of himself:

His knees suddenly bent, and you reached forward to put a hand beneath his elbow. And I, watching closely, felt with you your flicker of anticipation, your wish to move him aside so your charges could board the bus, your desire to leave this Indian—your fellow Westerner—some dignity. Oh, I moved through you, understanding all this and more, and it came to me that love is not an e-motion, an assertive putting out, but a *trans*-motion, a compliant moving through.

As if reflecting this example, Marshfield's diary shows his growing concern for others in his attitude toward the other clergymen at the retreat. Early in the diary Marshfield describes clergymen as "a cloying, pitiable, mean-spirited, earth-bound, repetitive lot." The first half of the diary, which is devoted entirely to Marshfield himself, scarcely mentions the other clergymen at the center. But he gradually becomes more aware of them and their problems, as he plays golf or card games with them and listens to their stories. He responds to them sympathetically and attempts to help them; "I longed to touch and heal," he tells us. As he reflects on a homosexual clergyman he invokes the person who formerly embodied for him the most hated of ethically oriented believers, his wife's father: "What is, old Professor Chillingworth asked through me, the good here mistakenly aspired to?"

Marshfield's last sermon is an attempt to comfort these fellow clergymen. In this function, it brings together the formerly separate, mutually exclusive concerns of faith and good works, of the supernatural and the natural. But the final sermon also attempts to join body and soul. As his first step in their integration, Marshfield discusses their indivisibility not in life but in death. About the afterlife he writes, "we do not want to live as angels in ether;

our bodies are us, us." It is, he continues, the hope of the resurrection of the body that brings people to church, yet paradoxically, "the resurrection of the body is impossible." We cannot believe it, "We can only *profess* to believe," and it is the clergyman's function "to be visible and to provide men with the opportunity to profess the impossible that makes their lives possible." Thus we see Marshfield not only recognizing the inseparability of body and soul but also transferring this understanding into a new sympathy with the human condition and a new dedication to the role of minister as helper.

It is at the end of this sermon that Ms. Prynne, sensing the integration of the formerly warring fragments of Marshfield's personality, writes, "Yes—at last, a sermon that could be preached." In the following entries Marshfield begs her to visit his room, for she has become, for him, the universal female figure, the "matrix of us all," the guide who, through the wholeness of her personality, has led him to wholeness, even in the desert.

The lack of particularization in the characterization of all the women in the novel, but most especially Ms. Prynne, allows them to become representative. Alicia represents only the physical to Marshfield and to us, Jane is entirely ethical, Mrs. Harlow totally spiritual. In his relationships with each of them important components of his personality were repudiated. But union with Ms. Prynne would represent Marshfield's victory over the former fragmentation of his personality. While Alicia made prayer impossible for Marshfield, when daydreaming of Ms. Prynne he alternately masturbates and prays; he has learned, finally, that "our acts, every one, are homage."

Ms. Prynne's name reinforces her role as a general representative of American womanhood, for it evokes the memory of Hester Prynne, main character in Hawthorne's *The Scarlet Letter*. In that novel, Hester Prynne was sentenced to wear a scarlet letter *A* as punishment

for her adultery. But in the character of the twentieth-
century Ms. Prynne, Updike has revised the traditional
guilt, the separation of physical desire from religious
experience, that Hester's scarlet letter carried. The twentieth-century Ms. Prynne wears no scarlet letter, but
rather joins her body willingly with our spokesman on
the last page of the novel.

The physical consummation that ends the novel
shows Marshfield reaching out to Ms. Prynne in wholeness and in joy. There is a feeling of communion in this
act that is rare in the usually isolationist world of the
Updike individual, alone even in sexual union. As they
make love, Marshfield writes that Ms. Prynne's expression
is one "of salutation," and "I pray my own face . . .
saluted in turn." By praying at this moment Marshfield
reveals his new wholeness.

Thus, at the end of *A Month of Sundays* Marshfield
rejects neither body for soul nor soul for body and is
able to profess faith in another world while he acts
ethically, and sympathetically, toward others in this world.
Early in the novel Marshfield talks of being interested in
"not the good but the godly. Not living well, but living
forever." At the end of the novel he realizes these are
not mutually exclusive possibilities.

Marshfield's progress is reflected in the style of his
diary entries. At first his word choice is self-consciously
witty, almost glib, with frequent puns, typographical er-
rors left to amuse the reader, and explanatory footnotes.
While these are amusing they also reveal Marshfield's
discomfort and defensive attitude toward his subject, himself. Marshfield's use of the third person when referring
to himself also reveals his anxiety; for example, he writes
about "our leading character, Tom." He distances himself
as well from other characters; they are "dolls I can play
with, putting them now in this, now in that obscene position." But as the month continues, Marshfield's wordplay
lessens and his treatment of other characters, both in the

past and present, becomes kinder. They are human be-
ings, not "dolls" or "puppets" whom he manipulates.

Marshfield's self-conscious wordplay and footnotes to
the reader also serve Updike's purpose of drawing the
reader into the drama of this novel. Marshfield con-
tinually addresses the reader and tries to outguess the
reader's possible psychological interpretations of his actions. This reader is both us and Ms. Prynne; we are,
combined, the "ideal reader" whom Marshfield constantly
addresses in his entries. He repeatedly addresses her, and
us, as "you insatiable reader, you," and he sees "your
blue pencil, Ideal Reader," poised to make corrections
and interpretations. Thus he makes us, as readers, believe
that we are somehow influencing what is written.

At the end of *A Month of Sundays* the reader is
brought into dismayingly close contact with the writer.
After the physical union Marshfield writes that there is
"nothing left for me to do, dear Ideal Reader, but slip
and topple off, gratefully," and so he ends the novel.
Surely this is the climax of a reciprocal relationship between writer and reader, and the increasing closeness
with the reader is evidence of, and corresponds to, Marshfield's increasing awareness of others and his attempts
to communicate with them.

The identification that occurs throughout the novel
of the reader with Ms. Prynne is appropriate thematically
as well. As Americans, we have all been influenced by
Hester Prynne and the separation of body and soul that
her scarlet letter represents. I have said that Ms. Prynne's
union with Marshfield is a symbolic rejection of Hester
Prynne's guilt and the scarlet letter that symbolizes it.
In *The Scarlet Letter* the preacher Dimmesdale reinforces
the body-soul division and the guilt which accompanies
it. Marshfield is the contemporary American preacher,
trying to unite these separated aspects of our religious
heritage. He writes that he is trying to recover "some
baggage lost in the Atlantic crossing," having to do with

"the acceptance of body by soul." It is "an American mystery," as is *The Scarlet Letter*. In referring to *The Scarlet Letter* with the names of both Ms. Prynne and Professor Chillingworth, Updike makes us aware of his purpose—to reject that separation of body and soul, of faith from good works, which is our heritage, and which was most popularly and influentially perpetuated in the novel.

Thus, I would argue that *A Month of Sundays* attempts to redefine our religious heritage by creating a paradigm of the contemporary religious scene in America. By a paradigm I mean that the symbolic action of the novel traces the movements that Updike feels have taken place in America's religious history. If we look at the novel in this way, Marshfield's progression among various women epitomizes the large movements of American religious history. Beginning with a long devotion, or marriage, to ethical action alone (Jane), it moves to a brief hedonism (Alicia), to a commitment to other-worldly faith devoid of physical action (Mrs. Harlow), and finally to a unification of them all (Ms. Prynne).

The symbolic treatment of the desert and the omega both serve to reinforce my theory that Updike intends for us to see this as a paradigm of American religious history. The desert is the vast, at first glance meaningless and empty, post-Wasteland world to which we have come from the lush greenery of New England. The desert is, Marshfield realizes, our real environment, and it is growing rapidly, so that even the White House is inhabited by a scorpion. Marshfield writes, "the special world of God within the Bible is an oasis world; the world beyond, the world of the Lord's wider creation, is a desert." It is this world, this desert world, in which he learns to live.

Within the desert that Tom Marshfield is sent to lies the omega-shaped resort for erring clergymen. The shape of the omega, like a man's head and shoulders, reminds us that the whole of the action of this novel takes place, at the very first level, within the head of Tom Marshfield. In another sense, the shelter is Ms. Prynne's Omega, the end of a long process of history that began with Hester Prynne's scarlet Alpha. For Updike seems to feel that the peculiarly American division of body from soul in religion and the guilt which accompanies it have at long last reached their end.

9

Marry Me

When *Marry Me* was published in 1976 most reviewers found it repetitive, for it relies on characters, situations, and themes that Updike has dealt with, more effectively, in earlier works. But while *Marry Me* remains unexceptional thematically, technically it shows originality and unusual experimentation.

Among these technical innovations is Updike's exclusive concentration on only four characters, with each of the first four sections of the novel dealing with events primarily from one character's point of view. Tension is created by this unrelenting focus on a quartet of characters who seem to compose a small universe among themselves. More important, tension is created by the main character's unfulfilled expectation of an important event, a sign from God. Waiting for God to act, the protagonist does not act himself. He is, throughout the novel, irresolute and indecisive. The technical device that Updike uses to reflect this indecision is presenting three possible conclusions to the novel.

The four characters in the novel are Jerry, the protagonist; Ruth, his wife; Sally, his mistress; and Richard, her husband. The first section of the novel is short and lyrical. It describes, from Jerry's point of view, his meeting on the beach with Sally, their communionlike drinking of wine, their lovemaking, and their misery at parting and returning to their respective spouses. Yet they are unwilling to upset their legal partners by asking for divorce. Jerry tells Sally that Ruth has been a "good wife," and does not deserve rejection.

The second, and much longer section, is told primarily from Sally's viewpoint. When Jerry phones from the airport to say goodbye before his two-day business trip to Washington, she cannot bear the separation. She leaves her children with a sitter, writes a note to Richard saying she must visit friends, and flies to Washington to meet Jerry.

During their night together we learn much more about Jerry and Sally. Jerry "believed in God" and confuses Sally by staring at the wall and "murmuring about pain and sin." On the other hand, Sally, a Catholic, has become so obsessed with Jerry that now "she didn't even know if she believed in God or not." She is untroubled by guilt for their affair, while Jerry seems almost to enjoy his conscience-stricken state. "It *would* be wonderful," he admits of her plan that they run off to Wyoming together, "if I could swallow the guilt."

Jerry endured insomnia and depression from his terrible fear of death before his affair with Sally, but now he feels alive; the sensuality and the nagging of his conscience both assure him of his existence. Sally wonders "if that was why Jerry had taken her into his life, to be taught about suffering." Indeed, to her, he complicates matters and suffers unnecessarily; he tells her at one point, "To live without you is death to me. On the other hand, to abandon my family is a sin; to do it I'd have to deny God, and by denying God I'd give up all claim on immortality." Sally, listening, can "hardly believe that minds still existed in that frame."

The most effective scene in the novel takes place at the airport where, their flight having been delayed and then cancelled, Jerry rushes around, frantically attempting to make alternate reservations or rent a car to get them home while keeping their affair undetected. But when all avenues of escape seem shut, Jerry decides their delay is an act of God. He proposes to Sally, saying he will divorce Ruth. While Sally is accepting the proposal, the airline attendant interrupts to announce that she has been able to get them on a flight home, leaving immediately. Jerry eagerly accepts. They fly home, and he is the first off the plane into the arms of Ruth, who has been waiting for hours. He hustles Ruth out of the airport so that she will not see Sally getting off the plane.

The third section of the novel shows Updike's rare sympathy and understanding of a female character. Entitled "The Reacting of Ruth," it portrays Jerry's wife's gradual realization that her husband prefers another woman, her shock, her hurt pride, her confusion, and her patient struggle to regain him.

Like Updike's first wife, Ruth is the daughter of a Unitarian minister, and her lack of religious fervor has been a sore point in their marriage. Jerry goes to church, teaches the children prayers, says grace before meals, and goes through periods of depression and fear of death that are meaningless to her. When Ruth tells Jerry that death does not frighten her, he tells her that she's "a spiritual cripple," that she's not afraid because she has "no imagination" and "no soul." "Once, wakened from sleep to hear him protest that one day he would die, Ruth had said 'Dust to dust,' and rolled over and gone back to sleep. Jerry never forgave this."

We learn that Ruth, in the previous year, had drifted in and out of her first affair. Her lover was Richard, Sally's husband. Never really loving him but pressed into the affair by his domination, she broke it off because of her concern that she was jeopardizing her marriage. Jerry, involved in his own fear of death, and then his affair with Sally, noticed neither Ruth's preoccupation during her affair nor her return to fidelity.

On the Sunday after his trip to Washington, Jerry, infecting his whole family with domestic discontent, fi-

nally tells Ruth that he wants to end their marriage. Full
of resentment that the rest of the family is sitting at the
dinner table in bathing suits while he, who has been to
church, wears a suit and tie, furious at being interrupted
during grace by three-year-old Geoffrey, Jerry slaps the
child, initiating one of Updike's few scenes of domestic
violence. When Ruth protests that the child does not
understand the difference between grace and prayers,
Jerry counters, "Then why the fuck don't you teach him?
If he had any decent even half-ass Christian kind of
mother he'd know enough not to interrupt." When the
child continues sobbing, his older brother hits him, and
his sister teases him. When Ruth attempts to hit Jerry,
he calls her a "pathetic frigid bitch."

In the aftermath of this turmoil Jerry reveals his
affair with Sally and his desire to leave Ruth. Yet, when
the evening is over he tells Ruth, "I don't know what to
do . . . I can't give either of you up." He promises Ruth
that he will attempt to renew his relationship with her,
avoiding all contact with Sally until the end of the
summer.

The series of confrontations that follow, between
Ruth and Sally, Ruth and Jerry, and Ruth and Richard
(who is still unaware of his wife's affair), are all told
from Ruth's perspective and show her desperate attempts
to win Jerry back. She tells Jerry, "You both seem to
think it's terribly unkind of me not to drop dead." Indeed, when Ruth, in one frantic drive, crashes her car,
she believes Jerry is disappointed that she wasn't killed.
He denies this, but does admit that "I've been waiting,
I suppose, for God to do something and this was it. His
way of saying that nothing is going to happen. Unless
you and I make it happen."

Ruth begins drinking, tense and depressed by Jerry's
ambivalence. She senses that he is still seeing Sally, in
spite of his agreement not to. At one point he tells her
that he is leaving, and she, relieved that he has finally

made a decision, accepts it. When he confronts the accusations and grief of his six-year-old son, Jerry changes
his mind, but he does finally move out of the house.

A few days later, Ruth suspects she is pregnant. She
gamely suggests an abortion, but for Jerry this pregnancy
is finally the word of God: "I've been waiting for an act
of God and this is it," he tells Ruth. He decides to forget
Sally and returns to his family. The next morning Ruth's
period starts; she is not pregnant after all.

The fourth section of the novel concentrates on Richard's reactions when he discovers his wife's affair. Richard
is a man of action, in contrast to Jerry, whose mode is
vacillation and ambivalence. An atheist, Richard does not
wait around for "an act of God"; instead he acts immediately and decisively. As soon as his suspicions concerning the affair are verified by Sally, he phones Ruth
and Jerry, summoning them to his house, telling them the
terms of the divorce he now insists upon. The meeting
of all four characters and their drinking together seem
almost ceremonial to Jerry.

Richard cannot understand Jerry's lack of action:

"But for Chrissakes, Jerry, you should've either broken it off
or run off with her. You put that woman through hell. You've
put—my wife—through hell. . . ."
Jerry shrugged. "I have a wife too."
"Well you have to pick. In our society you have to pick."

Richard moves out of his house that evening, contacts a
lawyer the next morning, and puts Ruth in touch with a
lawyer as well.

But events are moving too quickly for Jerry. Now
that his wife has gone to a divorce lawyer, now that his
mistress's husband is discussing settlements, he is having
second thoughts. The action is being controlled not by
God but by the atheist, Richard. Jerry decides not to get
a divorce after all. Yet as soon as he makes this decision
he finds Sally increasingly attractive, telling her, "Now

that you're no longer mine, all my old love has come pouring back."

Ruth takes Jerry back, telling him, "I may love you, Jerry, I don't know, but I have very little respect for you right now." Richard, too, takes Sally back. But he is furious with Jerry and promises him, "I'm going to make you pay." This threat brings Jerry a curious satisfaction; being hated "was a way, he saw, of being alive."

The last section of the novel, told from Jerry's point of view, presents the reader with three possible conclusions. In the first ending, Jerry and Sally and her children go to Wyoming. In the second, Jerry, Ruth, and their children go to France. In the third, Jerry goes on a trip alone to St. Croix. The equivocation created by these three endings reflects the irresolution of the protagonist throughout the novel. Even in the conclusion of the novel he is uncertain of which woman to choose, which direction his life should follow.

In the first conclusion, when he is with Sally, Jerry is nagged by guilt and memories of Ruth and Richard. He tries to placate Sally's demanding children and is criticized in his handling of them by Sally. In the second conclusion, when he is with Ruth, Jerry is unable to stop thinking of Sally. But the third conclusion, Jerry's trip alone, is full of clear mountain air, breathtaking vistas, and ambiguous religious references. Alone on an island, Jerry feels "intensely, passingly happy."

This happiness is only possible when Jerry is alone, not tied down to any one woman. Women are too limited to breathe the rare air of the heights in St. Croix. Women in this novel, as with almost all of Updike's female characters, are practical and unimaginative. Sally explains to Jerry, "Women try to be like men, Jerry, and imagine things, but in the end we're all practical, we have to be. You must go on alone."

The characterization of Ruth reflects this portrayal of women as unimaginative and therefore untroubled by metaphysical anxieties. Jerry tells Ruth at one point that, unlike him, "what's impossible doesn't interest you. Your eyes just don't see it." She doesn't understand Jerry's dread of death, and she accepts the natural cycle with equanimity.

Being spiritually earthbound, Ruth is repeatedly associated with the earth throughout the novel. Sex with Ruth is, for Jerry, "a roll in the mud." She lands her car in a sodden, muddy ditch. During their affair she and Richard drive down a dirt road to an inland pond; as they kiss, the soggy soil seeps through Ruth's shoes. In fact the whole affair between the Unitarian and the atheist is limited and inadequate, reflected in the shallow attachment of each for the other.

On the other hand, lovemaking between Sally and Jerry occurs by the deep and limitless ocean. They don't drive on the ground, they fly in the air. During their flight Jerry's description of Sally and his feelings for her becomes an incredibly lyrical hymn of praise. Thus their flight is a kind of ascension for Jerry. But Sally is unconscious of the heights; she sleeps through the flight and only awakens when they land on the ground.

Part of Sally's attraction for Jerry is that she is married to Richard, whom Jerry hates. As an atheist, Richard has often mocked Jerry's religious intensity. At a party years before, Richard had produced "a plastic dashboard Christ that had arrived unsolicited in the mails, and proceeded to clean his fingernails with the tip of the hand upraised in blessing. 'Look, Sally-O,' he had said, 'doesn't Christ make a good fingernail-picker?' " Jerry never forgot this incident. He calls Richard, on various occasions, a "bad man," "an ogre," and "a spiritual cripple." The women in the novel are of course insensitive to Richard's evil, but Jerry imagines Sally as "a princess married to an ogre," and he is the knight who must rescue her. "With the sword of his flesh he had put the mockers to rout. Christ was revenged."

Updike's opinion of Richard's atheism is reflected in the fact that he has made Richard blind in one eye. At one point Jerry "wondered what it would be like to see with only one eye." Covering one eye, he decides that everything around him "invisibly shed a dimension. Things were just so, flat, with nothing further to be said about them; it was the world, he realized, as seen without the idea of God lending each thing a roundness of significance. It was terrible."

In this world of spiritual uncertainty "men don't like to make decisions," Jerry tells us, "they want God or women to make them." Women, undisturbed by visions of the other world, expect their "gods," the men, to make decisions. They cannot understand that Jerry's irresolution is the result of his desperate awareness of living "in the twilight of the old morality, and there's just enough to torment us, and not enough to hold us in."

10

The Coup

Updike's *The Coup* was published to rave reviews in the fall of 1978, becoming an immediate best-seller and a Book-of-the-Month Club selection. At first glance this novel is an entirely new departure for Updike. Its setting is mostly African, not American, its protagonist is a black Islamic Marxist, not a WASP, and it quotes the Koran, not the Bible. In 1973, on a lecture tour for the State Department, Updike saw the sub-Saharan countries in the midst of a terrible drought. Updike has transformed this experience into a novel that combines satirical thrusts at the United States with a recognition of the cultural values of the third world. He has created a disarming and engaging protagonist who, in telling his story, joins the fantastic with the realistic, the grotesque with the ridiculous, in a manner that is both delightfully entertaining and enlightening.

The protagonist and putative author of *The Coup* is Félix Ellelloû, former President of the landlocked, impoverished African nation of Kush. Kush is largely Saharan desert. It has a single brown and sluggish river, and although it is larger than any two nations of Europe, it has only 22 miles of railroad, 107 miles of paved highway, and a national airline (Air Kush) with two antiquated planes. Its chief natural resource, Ellelloû tells us, is a superfluity of diseases such as malaria, typhus, sleeping sickness, leprosy, and yaws. The average life expectancy is thirty-seven, the average income is seventy-

nine dollars per annum, and the literacy rate is six percent. We might call it the most backward of African
nations, yet Ellelloû loves the land of Kush above all else;
he cherishes its emptiness and lack of progress.

The Coup is presented as Ellelloû's memoirs. During
the course of the novel we learn that he was born in 1933,
the result of the rape of a tribal woman by a raider.
Scorned in his village because of his illegitimacy, Ellelloû
left at seventeen to fight for the French in Indochina.
(Kush was, at that time, still a colony of France.) When,
in 1954, France began fighting in Algeria, Ellelloû re-
fused to fight fellow Africans, deserted, and became a
rebel. For his own safety he fled to the United States
where, supported by a meagre scholarship and odd jobs,
he studied at McCarthy College in Franchise, Wisconsin.

By the time Kush became independent in 1960,
Ellelloû had returned to Kush as attaché to the constitu-
tional monarch, King Edumu IV. In 1968 he was involved in a successful plot to overthrow and imprison
the king. Shortly after, Ellelloû became president. Ellelloû's presidency was supposed to introduce a Marxist
revolution, but as Ellelloû tells us, the revolutionaries
found nothing to nationalize in a country without in-
dustry, natural resources, transportation or communication networks. Nonetheless Ellelloû honors the ideals of
"Islamic Marxism," looking upon anything American as
a threat to his country.

The main action of the novel occurs in 1973. Ellelloû has been president for five years, during which an
unprecedented drought has descended on the already
parched land. There is terrible starvation. The United
States, moved by the suffering, and perhaps sensing a
political advantage to be gained, has sent supplies that
sit on the northern border of Kush in the care of an AID
agent. Ellelloû has neither the desire nor the means to
distribute the foodstuffs to his people, but their presence
on his border bothers him.

In the opening section of the novel Ellelloû travels
by camel and caravan to these American donations. He
finds a pyramid of crates piled in the endless desert,
stamped "USA USA USA USA," and "Kix Trix," "Chex
Pops," or "Korn Kurls." Ellelloû asks about the "mountain of refuse," but the agent, Donald Gibbs, objects,
saying, "This isn't refuse, pal—it's manna" for "the prim-
itives." But Ellelloû rejects "capitalist intervention," as-
serting that the Kushites "have no place in their stomachs
for the table scraps of a society both godless and op-
pressive." Gibbs argues that it is not *all* junk food, bringing the Carnation dry milk to Ellelloû's attention: "add
three parts water," he directs. "But we have no water!"
counters Ellelloû. Attempting a hard sell, the American
climbs higher and higher on the pyramid of crates,
frantically tossing down samples to Ellelloû. When he
reaches the pinnacle, Ellelloû touches the torches of his
followers to the cartons, making them Gibbs's funeral
pyre.

When he returns to the capital Ellelloû is deeply
troubled by the starvation he has seen. Feeling responsible for the prolonged drought that began when he
assumed his presidency, he decides he must behead the
imprisoned king, hoping that this violent act will appease
Allah and bring rain. The king, old and blind, had trusted
Ellelloû years before and raised him to a position of
power. But he had also ruled the country as a selfish
monarch, with "the unexamined assumption that he was
right to demand and consume what so many strained to
donate out of their poverty."

A mock trial is staged, and Ellelloû himself decapi-
tates the king at a public execution, holding the head
he loves aloft for his audience to see. Masked horsemen
appear and wrench the head from Ellelloû's hands. Weeks
later Ellelloû hears rumors that the king's head is talking
prophecies in a cave deep in the desert. The people are
flocking to this miracle, and Ellelloû decides he must go

on a pilgrimage through the desert to hear the oracle himself. His purpose is "to purify his life and redeem his land."

But before he leaves, Ellellou must deal with his chief adviser, Michael Ezana, a practical opportunist who shares none of Ellellou's distrust of the United States. Ezana believes that Kush can only benefit from American involvement. The contrast between these two characters and their opposing political philosophies is central to the novel. While Ezana wishes to accept American scientific, agricultural, industrial, and financial aid to reduce suffering in Kush, Ellellou tells him to "Forget the infidels, they are mired in materialism and its swinish extinction of spirit." While Ezana believes that without American recognition "we cease to exist in the world," Ellellou believes that they would therefore "begin to exist in a better world." Ezana is impatient with Ellellou's mysticism. He tells the president, "There is no way a nation cannot live in the world. A man, yes, can withdraw into sainthood; but a nation, of its very collective essence, strives to prosper."

Believing this, Ezana, against Ellellou's orders, has begun negotiations with Klipspringer, the U.S. Undersecretary of State, in response to his inquiry concerning the disappearance of Gibbs and the American supplies. Apprised of Ezana's betrayal of his authority, Ellellou imprisons Ezana and prepares to visit the oracle.

Before leaving, Ellellou visits the second of his four wives, Candy, an American from his undergraduate days in Wisconsin. She is his prisoner, kept heavily veiled and carefully watched when she goes out, so that few know the president has an American wife. Perhaps it is this brief and discordant visit that prompts Ellellou to reminisce about his years in the States as he travels to the oracle. He remembers undergraduate life in the American Midwest, football games and beer kegs, soda fountains and Patti Page, falling leaves, classes skipped, making

love with Candy. But it was also during these years that
Ellelloû became a devout Muslim. He was taken by an
American Black Muslim to meetings of the Nation of
Islam in Chicago where the Messenger of Allah taught
him "that the world is our enslaver and that the path to
freedom is the path of abnegation."

Ellelloû is on "the path of abnegation" as he travels
through the hot, dry desert. His progress is slow and
painful. He travels first by camel; when the camels die
of thirst, Ellelloû drinks their blood to relieve his own
thirst and continues on foot. But as Ellelloû approaches
the cave containing the prophetic head, he is astounded
to see, arising from the seemingly endless desert, a highway, tourist buses, signs and arrows to the "Oracle's
Cave," the litter of Popsicle wrappers, Coke stands, ticket
booths, and crowds of tourists.

Inside the cave the king's head is displayed on an
altar of transparent Plexiglas, demonstrating the absence
of a body. Suddenly the eyelids lift and the lips move
mechanically, telling the crowd that Ellelloû is "a greatly
evil man" who pretends to hate materialism and Americanism but secretly loves it. As proof of Ellelloû's par-
tiality to American materialism, the head directs its audience to an American boom town in Kush and ends its
message saying, "Overthrow Ellelloû and rain will fall!"

Enraged, Ellelloû rips the head from the Plexiglas
altar to expose a cranium full of mechanical apparatus
connected by transparent wires to a speaker. It is a Soviet
invention; the Russians are outraged by the American
town that has suddenly mushroomed in the desert. They
do not know it is not Ellelloû but Ezana who has had
the town built secretly.

Following the oracle's directions, Ellelloû proceeds
through the desert to the town. He finds a little America,
with gas stations and McDonalds, supermarkets and parking lots, suburbs with ranch houses, trailer parks and
go-go dives. The Africans in the town wear cowboy hats

and blue jeans and chew bubble gum. It is all supported by oil wells run by American oil companies.

Because he believes Kush will be "Xed out by Exxon, engulfed by Gulf," Ellelloû attempts to incite the populace to destroy the oil refineries. He urges the Kushites to set fire to the refineries, telling them "The conflagration will lighten your hearts forever, and become the subject of a song you can sing your grandchildren." But he is trampled by the crowd, which is distracted from his speech by the offer of free beer from the American directors.

At this point, when Ellelloû is powerless and believed trampled to death, rain begins to fall on Kush. Back in the capital Ezana has escaped, assumed power, and renewed negotiations with Klipspringer, who arrives in Kush full of clichés and good intentions. With American aid Ezana plans to urbanize the nomads, zone the villages for agribusiness, and create an industrial state. He christens the oil town "Gibbsville" in honor of the dead American agent.

By the time Ellelloû returns to the capital it remains only for him to go into exile. He wants to take with him at least one of his four wives. But Candy is divorcing him and returning to America. Ellelloû's first wife, a tribal woman, is dead, signifiying the extinction of tribal life under Ezana's Bureau of Detribalization. The third wife, burnt out while still a teenager from the constant chewing of hallucinogenic plants, has disappeared. But the fourth wife is a reflection of modern Africa; she paints and jogs, loves her country and distrusts America, has six children by Ellelloû and various lovers. She is delighted to accept Ellelloû's invitation to escape the Americanization of Kush. They go to the South of France where, supported by a pension from the government of Kush, Ellelloû writes his memoirs.

Through the character of Ellelloû Updike reveals the human dichotomy that has concerned him throughout his writing career. The body-spirit conflict is at the basis of

Ellelloû's anti-Americanism. He distrusts material goods
and physical comforts because they distract us from spiritual commitment. Thus the U.S.A. is "the land of the
devils" that both attracts and repels him. The oracular
head tells its audience that Ellelloû has "projected upon
the nation his own ambivalent will—American vs. African, carnal vs. spiritual." This ambivalence is reflected
in his choice of wives, including one American, who,
like his own fondness for America, he keeps hidden and
disguised.

Yet Ellelloû's disdain of the physical, the materialism
that America has come to represent to him, always pre-
vails. "Ellelloû" means "freedom," but Ellelloû defines
freedom as "the righteous disdain of that world which
Allah has cast forth as a vapor, a dream." He rules a
nation over which "materialism has yet to cast its full
spell," and his purpose is to save it from the "toubabs"
who "look into the microscope and tell us there is no
spirit."

Although the suffering he sees upsets him, the
drought is a fulfillment of the physical deprivation for
which Ellelloû yearns, so that the spirit may rise, unencumbered. The executed king tells Ellelloû: "The sky
spirit has come to hate the earth spirit. Your land is
cursed, unhappy Félix. You have cursed this land with
your hatred of the world."

Because of his distrust of material goods Ellelloû
envies the poor: "Their lives are a shabby anteroom in
the palace of the afterlife." They feel none of his painful
ambivalence because they are not tempted by material
comforts. In keeping with his beliefs, Ellelloû resists the
opulence the former king practiced. His diet is sparse,
his dress is plain, and he delights in appearing incognito;
he has none of the usual dictator's delight in pomp and
ostentation.

Yet all of this rejection of earthly temptation brings
Ellelloû little spiritual certainty. His faith has that ele-

ment of doubt that is always constant in Updike's fiction. He believes that "No fervor overtops that which arises from contact with the Absolute," but he recognizes that "the contact may be all one way." The desert stars cause him to reflect: "My life by those lunar perspectives became a focus of terror, an infinitely small point nevertheless enormously hollow." He fears and suspects that "we are less than dust in the scheme of things."

This doubt leads Ellelloû to the recognition of "the attenuation, dessication, and death of religions the world over." Yet out of this death, a

new religion is being formed in the indistinct hearts of men, a religion without a God, without prohibitions and compensatory assurances, a religion whose antipodes are motion and stasis, whose one rite is the exercise of energy, and in which exhausted forms like the quest, the vow, the expiation, and the attainment, through suffering, of wisdom are, emptied of content, put in the service of a pervasive expenditure whose ultimate purpose is entropy, whose immediate reward is fatigue, a blameless confusion, and sleep.

In the service of this religion, Ellelloû goes on his quest, knowing that the oracular head is a hoax yet taking comfort in his own enactment of the traditional ceremony of the pilgrimage.

In *The Coup* Updike has shown the inevitable capitulation of contemporary Third World countries to the materialism that the United States represents. Even when Ellelloû is leader of his country he cannot destroy the incipient Americanism that creeps across the borders of Kush. Although he rejects, and burns, Donald Gibbs and his "Korn Kurls," he cannot police a whole country whose populace has turned away from the traditional religion, entranced by the American way of life. The mosques in which Ellelloû prays are empty. Instead of praying, the Kushites listen to transistor radios that blare forth the latest hits from the American hit parade. Ellelloû's

adviser surreptitiously reads the latest American best-
seller and drinks Ovaltine. To Ellelloû's horror, his mistress has taken to wearing American lingerie, Playtex
bras and pantyhose. Ellelloû fights a losing battle in his
attempt to maintain the cultural purity of Kush.

His defeat by Ezana represents a victory for materialism and physical comfort, and the complete rejection of religion and the traditional way of life. Ezana is
no mystic; he tells Ellelloû, "The fading of an afterlife—
for it has faded, my friend Ellelloû, however you churn
your heart—has made this life more to be cherished."
Ezana plans to bring material and technological progress
to Kush, based on "Capital investments cleverly pried
from the rivalry between the two superpowers." This
prosperity will reduce the unnecessary suffering he sees
around him, and it will urbanize the villagers and the
nomads whose way of life Ezana calls "archaic, wasteful
and destructive."

Updike's stylistic range is more apparent in *The
Coup* than in any previous novel. In this novel, Updike's
metaphorical yet highly specific style, his often convoluted
sentences, strangely suit the African narrator to whom,
we know, English is a third language (after his tribal
tongue and the colonial French). Ellelloû's most private
thoughts and his descriptions of events are given this
lyrical, slightly stilted voice. He sings:

"A land without a conscience is an empty land, a blasted
land, a desert land."

His quotations from the Koran merge with this style, as
do his descriptions of the desert and its wild inhabitants:
"Drifting like clouds, the giraffes would canter away,
their distant mild faces unblaming, the orbs of their great
eyes more luminous than the moon."

But Updike's style changes to suit Ellelloû's purpose.
Here is the propaganda-filled pronouncement of Ellelloû
as dictator, announcing the king's execution:

The National Honor of Kush and the Will of Allah demand
that Justice be Done to this Reactionary and Discredited
Exploiter of the Many, who in the course of his Mockery of
a Reign appropriated to Himself the Means of Production
and the Headwaters of Revenue . . .

Most striking are Ellelloû's memories of America, in
which his style becomes satirically sharp, yet highly amusing. Here is his devastating description of Candy's adolescent brother, whom he remembers meeting in her living room in Franchise:

Frank Jr. was a furtive, semi-obese child of fourteen—old
enough, in my village, for the long house—whose complexion
showed the ravages of sleeping alone, night after night, in
an overheated room with teddy bears, felt pennants, and
dotted swiss curtains. The smile he grudged me displayed a
barbarous, no doubt painful tooth-armor of silver and steel.
His limp dank handshake savored of masturbatory rites. His
eyes were fishy with boredom, and he tried to talk to me
about basketball, of which I knew, despite my color, nothing.
For this family occasion the child had put on a shirt and
tie; the collar and knot cut cruelly into the doughy flesh of
his neck. I thought, Here is the inheritor of capitalism and
imperialism. . . .

Equally derisive is this list of titles that Ellelloû reads
from the bookshelves of Candy's personal library in
Africa:

How to succeed, how to be saved, how to survive the mid-life
crisis, how to find fulfillment within femininity, how to be
free, how to love, how to face death, how to harness your
fantasies, how to make dollars in your spare time—the endless self-help and self-exploration of a performance oriented
race that has never settled within itself the fundamental
question of what a man *is*.

There are moments when Ellelloû's style strikes an
emotional honesty, cutting through the satire and the
farce to reveal the troubled man beneath. For example,

as he recounts his beheading of the king, Ellelloû interrupts himself: "The very ink in my pen coagulates at
these memories."

When Updike moves to the dialogue of Americans
in the novel his style becomes colloquial and blunt, contrasting dramatically with the circumlocutions of the
Africans' speech. For example, Candy calls Ellelloû a "sa-
distic little turd." Gibbs assures Ellelloû that his breakfast cereals "are dynamite, don't knock 'em." The
rhetoric of Klipspringer is a marvelous parody of the
easily manipulated, incompetent American politician who
speaks in clichés. About the United States Klipspringer
asserts loyally, "It's the place for me," and he privately
tells Ezana that in this post-Watergate period Nixon
"looks like a loser, from where I sit." He encourages
Ezana to accept all the U.S. aid he is offered, because
"The deeper in debt the debtor gets, the more the creditor
will invest to keep them from going under." He is behind the United States "one hundred and ten percent,"
and the festivities arranged to entertain him in Kush are
"Kinda fun." He is, in his own words, "quite a character."

It is evidence of Updike's considerable talent that he
has gone beyond the confines of American life and created
a superb novel about Islamic Africa. Yet this African
novel is relevant to us all in the twentieth century. The
issues it confronts are those with which all thinking people struggle. The desert of Kush, its vast emptiness, its
potential meaninglessness, become an analogue for the
human condition. Quoting the Koran at the end of the
novel, Ellelloû tells us, "Allah is the master of every plot:
He knows the deserts of every soul." Updike has conveyed these deserts and their vast emptiness to us.

11

Some Short Stories

Updike received recognition first as a writer of short stories, and he has published almost as many collections of short stories as novels. Most of these stories were previously published in *The New Yorker* or some other magazine. Because of limitations of space, and because of the overwhelming number of Updike's short stories, I will be able only to generalize about them. I will then concentrate briefly on two of the most frequently anthologized short stories and one collection.

There are many similarities between Updike's short stories and his novels, and many of the observations that I have made about the novels hold true for the stories as well. As in the novels, the short stories are often concerned with how the natural world (whether evidenced by pigeons or sexual encounters) relates to the supernatural. A frequent theme in both genres is the consideration of social and familial obligations as sacrifice, resulting in a diminishing of the protagonist's artistic or religious or sexual freedom. The nostalgia for the past, the tenuousness of middle-class institutions, particularly marriage and the family, the suspicion that Updike has always had for what seems, on the surface, to be heroic and unselfish action, all these are frequent themes in the short stories.

In the short stories Updike concentrates not as much on the event as upon the effect of outward events upon the protagonist. While the same may be said of the novels, Updike realizes that as a genre, novels demand more action simply to sustain their length. Because of their brevity, the short stories can sustain uninterrupted introspection, a spareness of overt action, in a way that novels cannot. Thus the genre of the short story allows Updike to present selected and detailed vignettes focused on the nuances of the protagonist's reaction to events.

For those readers used to dime-store thrillers, the plots in the short stories may seem bare: in one a man takes his daughter to a music lesson, in another a father tells his child a bedtime story, in many the temptations toward or suspicions of adultery are suffered but seldom confirmed. Moreover, within the brevity of the short story, Updike's remarkable style, unfailingly precise, often lyrical, occasionally ironic, becomes even more noticeable than in the novels.

Perhaps the most sustained stylistic achievement in any of the short stories comes in the frequently anthologized story "Pigeon Feathers." David is the young protagonist, an adolescent who has been plunged into religious doubt by his almost accidental reading of H. G. Wells's account of Jesus. Wells describes Jesus as "an obscure political agitator, a kind of hobo, in a minor colony of the Roman Empire," who "by an accident impossible to reconstruct . . . survived his own crucifixion and presumably died a few weeks later." Outraged by the sacrilege of this account, David's first reaction is astonishment that the man who had written such "blasphemy" had not been struck by lightning but had been allowed to continue writing, "to grow old, win honors, wear a hat, write books that, if true, collapsed everything into a jumble of horror."

In the weeks following, David's doubt and depression grow, as does his sense of alienation from his family and acquaintances. This sense of alienation is reinforced by the fact that David is an only child who has just moved,

with his family, from town to farm. (These details cor-
respond to events in Updike's own adolescence). The nature he contemplates in the loneliness of the farm reminds
him of the persistence of death and decay in the natural
cycle. In the darkness of the outhouse one night, David
experiences a moment of consummate horror as he contemplates the possibility of his own death, without resurrection. He questions the minister during a church con-
firmation class but the other children laugh at his
impertinence, and the clergyman, answering, reveals his
own disbelief in the resurrection of each individual.

Weeks later, when David is asked by his mother to
shoot the pigeons who are fouling furniture stored in the
barn, he accepts the task with increasing eagerness. Since
the universe has been revealed to him as possibly uncaring, there has developed a streak of meanness within
David, a reflexive lack of caring. Into the darkness of
the barn comes the destroyer, with his new gun, a fif-
teenth birthday present. The pigeons are his helpless
victims.

In describing the pigeons, Updike's style becomes
lyrical and precise. The sound of their cooing "flooded
the vast interior with its throaty, bubbling outpour."
David aims at a pigeon that is "preening and cooing in
a throbbing, thrilled, tentative way" and shoots at its
"tiny, jauntily cocked head." The bird, "pirouetting rapidly and nodding its head as if in frantic agreement,"
finally falls. As the cooing of the remaining pigeons becomes shriller, their "apprehensive tremolo made the
whole volume of air seem liquid."

When David buries his victims, he notices, for the
first time, the intricate individual design of each bird.
The pattern of each feather is carefully and precisely
colored. Each feather is trimmed to fulfill its purpose.
One pigeon has plumage "slate shades of blue," another
is "mottled all over in rhythms of lilac and gray." David
becomes convinced that "the God who had lavished such

craft upon these worthless birds would not destroy His whole Creation by refusing to let David live forever."

There is irony, of course, in this final statement of the story. David thinks that the birds are worthless, although they have shown so much to him. Moreover, in the self-centered manner of adolescents, he believes the universe has been created for his own pleasure, and that his death would imply its destruction; thus, David concludes he will "live forever."

In the lyrical description of the birds, Updike frequently uses words associated with the arts, with music, with dancing, and in the burial scene, with painting. Words like "tremolo" and "pirouetting" and the detailed description of the color and pattern of the feathers reinforce Updike's ultimate purpose, to suggest the existence of a design, and thus a Designer, in the natural world. While philosophical objections could be (and have been) made to the argument of design as proof of God's existence, the tone of gentle irony in the final paragraph assures us of Updike's control of his theme. As Robert Detweiler writes:

The point is that Updike, through symbolic action and analogy, has written a moving religious narrative that does not presume to convince one of the objective truth of Christian faith, but that does testify to an individual's achievement of it.[1]

Updike's story "A & P" is perhaps his most popular; it has been anthologized in many college texts. "A & P" derives its impact from the narrative voice, comic contrast, and the ironic distance between the intentions of the protagonist and what he actually accomplishes.

Sammy, the narrator, is a nineteen-year-old checkout clerk at an A & P market in a New England town that is close to a wealthy beach colony. The narrative voice is established immediately as familiar and colloquial, using the present tense for dramatic impact; it is as if the young narrator is recounting the incident to a friend. "In walks these three girls in nothing but bathing suits," he begins. "I'm in the third checkout slot, with my back to the door, so I don't see them until they're over by the bread."

Much of the humor in the story comes from Sammy's response to the girls. Mesmerized by his initial sight of them, he rings up "a box of HiHo crackers" twice, enraging his customer. When the girls come into view again, Sammy's attention becomes fixed on the "queen" of the three. She walks with poised nonchalance, barefoot, with the straps of her bathing suit off her shoulders; "as a result the suit had slipped a little on her," Sammy tells us, to reveal where her tan ends. She leads the other girls down one aisle, to the meat counter, and up another aisle, appearing by the checkout lanes with a jar of "Fancy Herring Snacks in Pure Sour Cream." They come to Sammy's lane, and from the "hollow at the center of her nubbled pink" bathing suit top, the queen lifts a folded dollar. As Sammy watches this maneuver he tells us, "The jar went heavy in my hand."

At this point the manager of the store appears. Lengel, a Sunday school teacher, is affronted by the indignity of the girls shopping in his store in such attire. "We want you decently dressed when you come in here," he tells the girls, who blush, suddenly embarrassed. Enraged that Lengel has humiliated the girls, Sammy says, " 'I quit' . . . quick enough for them to hear, hoping they'll stop and watch me, their unsuspected hero." But the girls "keep right on going," and Sammy is left to carry out his heroic gesture, remove his apron and his bow tie, ring up No Sale on the register, and leave, jobless and alone. The final sentence registers Sammy's awareness of "how hard the world was going to be for me hereafter."

The irony of Sammy's heroism reflects Updike's conviction, obvious in many of his works, that the heroic gesture is often meaningless and usually arises from selfish

rather than unselfish impulses. Sammy wants to be noticed by the girls, but he isn't. They are of a social class
beyond his, for he is a town boy, they are summer
vacationers, from families who snack on herring in sour
cream as they sip their cocktails. Sammy is aware of the
gulf between them; the only way he can get them to
notice him is to differentiate himself from what he sees,
through their eyes, as the hopeless provincialism of the
small town that insists on "decent dress" in its supermarkets. When the manager rebukes the girls, "Queenie"
(as Sammy calls the leader), begins to get "sore now
that she remembers her place, a place from which the
crowd that runs the A & P must look pretty crummy.
Fancy Herring Snacks flashed in her very blue eyes."

But the comic tone of the story is also created by
the contrast between the usual customers at the A & P
and these girls. Sammy is painfully aware of female
appearances, and he describes the matrons he sees daily
on his job in terms that are representative of his age
group. There is a "witch about fifty with rouge on her
cheekbones and no eyebrows" who screeches when he
rings up her purchase twice. There are "a few house-
slaves in pin curlers." There is "an old party in baggy
gray pants" buying four giant cans of pineapple juice,
and there are "women with six children and varicose
veins mapping their legs." They are described repeatedly
as "sheep" who are "pushing their carts down the aisle."
When Sammy closes down his register and quits, he tells
us the middle-aged matrons knock against each other
to get to another checkout counter "like scared pigs in
a chute."

On the other hand, the three girls, and especially
the queen, are described in intimate and pleasurable detail. The queen has "long white prima-donna legs," and
"oaky hair that the sun and salt had bleached." But to
prevent the story from becoming maudlin, Updike often
uses Sammy's youthful and unromantic descriptive pow-

ers. The dollar bill that the girl lifts from her cleavage is uncreased by Sammy "tenderly as you may imagine, it just having come from between the two smoothest scoops of vanilla I had ever known. . . ." As he waits breathlessly at the checkout for the girls to appear from one of the aisles, Sammy describes "the whole store" as being "like a pinball machine and I didn't know which tunnel they'd come out of." The maudlin is also prevented by Updike's precise eye for detail; there is no soft-focused romanticism here. The girls appear against a background of "Diet Delight peaches," stacked dog food, packaged spaghetti, and cheap plastic toys.

Sammy's quitting has been described, by one critic, as "the reflex of the still uncorrupted, of the youth still capable of the grand gesture because he has not learned the sad wisdom of compromise." [2] Sammy's loneliness at the end of the story is the result of this gesture: the girls have taken no notice of him, but he has alienated himself from the town by presuming to judge its standards.

The short stories by Updike that are most familiar to readers of *The New Yorker* are the seventeen that trace the history and eventual dissolution of the marriage of Joan and Dick Maple. In 1979 these were collected into a volume entitled *Too Far To Go* [3] and made into a television movie of the same title. The stories, written over a span of twenty-three years, follow the outward events of Updike's own first marriage: Dick Maple, like Updike, married in the early fifties when he was twenty-one; both couples had four children, separated after twenty-one years, and finally received one of the first no-fault divorces granted in the state of Massachusetts.

Most of the Maple stories are told from the point of view of Dick Maple who, like many of Updike's pro-tagonists, suffers insomnia and frequent minor illnesses (a nervous stomach in Rome, a mysterious fever the day of a civil rights demonstration, innumerable colds). He recognizes that these are possibly psychosomatic, as his

128   John Updike

doctor suggests in the final story. These illnesses reflect
Dick Maple's uneasy relationship with his own body;
when it is not irritating him with illness, it plagues him
with sexual hungers. His character reveals an uncomfortable conjunction of independence and insecurity, both
aggravated not so much by his wife as by his married
state.

In contrast, Joan Maple is revealed in these stories
as being, for the most part, competent and conscientious.
Dick finds her mysterious and distant, describing her as
"solid but hidden," and finally, as "a secret woman he
could never reach and had at last wearied of trying to
reach." In the early stories she is clearly in control. In
"Wife-Wooing" she refuses her husband's advances only
to initiate sex with him the next night, when he is not
expecting it. In the next story, "Giving Blood," several
years and one child later, she has convinced Richard,
over his squeamish objections, to go to Boston with her
to give blood for her cousin who is ill.

But in this story there is a new note of friction in
the marriage. During the drive to Boston each accuses
the other of flirting at a party the night before. Dick
coolly accuses Joan of smugness and sexlessness. But joined
by the strange sacrificial ceremony of giving blood, they
make peace over the late breakfast in a restaurant, with
Dick pretending that he is Joan's romantic suitor on a
date until he finds his wallet empty and must take money
from his wife.

Subsequent stories show them drawing further apart.
They "had talked and thought about separation," but
their "conversations, increasingly ambivalent and ruthless
as accusation, retraction, blow and caress alternated and
canceled, had the final effect of knitting them ever tighter
together in a painful, helpless, degrading intimacy." One
story centers on a mysterious telephone caller; each accuses the other that it must be his or her lover. In another, Dick warmly embraces a divorced woman whom

he and Joan have been driving home from a party, and in another, he comes upon his wife and a mutual friend embracing in the kitchen of his house.

The accusations and suppositions, Dick's occasional attraction to his wife, and his frequent rejection of her continue through the stories. It is like an elaborate dance in which, pledged to keep each other as partners, the couple, perhaps because of this enforced commitment, draws farther and farther apart. The concentration in these stories is always on the couple; lovers remain shadowy background figures whose implied presence is incidental and not the cause of the distance between the couple.

It is ironic that this distance, rather than closeness, is the end result of so many, ultimately futile, conversations. The Maples talk endlessly over the years, but all these words fail to draw them closer. Thus, one of the effects of these stories is to demonstrate the limitations of words as a means of communication, as the writer depends on them to convey this message to the reader.

After twenty-one years of marriage, the Maples do decide to separate, and the story "Separating" records their painful breaking of the news to their children, now young adults and adolescents. Dick and Joan, concerned about the effect of the news they feel they must inflict upon the children, have waited months for the right moment. But, as one critic puts it, "there turns out to be no proper moment for such a revelation." [4] While the girls respond with a quiet stoicism, the younger son at first shouts at his parents accusingly, then jokes, and then dissolves in tears in a scene that rings painfully true. The older son seems to accept the separation with calm, yet as he kisses his father good night he moans in his ear the unanswerable question, "Why?"

Perhaps the Maples' closest moment is, ironically, in the courthouse right after their divorce is legalized. The final story of the volume, "Here Come the Maples,"

links Richard's memories of his wedding with the formali-
ties and red tape of getting a divorce. He must get a copy
of their marriage license, and in doing so, Dick finds
himself remembering, with increasing detail, his wedding
day, the day they began what they are now about to end.
When the Maples arrive in court they are as nervous as
any young bride and groom, although their marriage is
about to be dissolved, not solemnized. To the judge's
questions Dick and Joan answer, "I do," echoing the
marriage ceremony. As the ceremony ends, Dick turns to
his former wife and kisses her, remembering to do what,
twenty-two years before at their wedding ceremony, he
had forgotten.

In her review of the Maple stories Erica Jong has
written, "Their separation and divorce are the more
poignant for their not hating each other. The title of this
collection might well be 'No Fault.' " [5] In the Maple
stories Updike has succeeded in being impartial and unblaming. It is always much easier to blame than to understand, and yet Updike has avoided this temptation. Out
of his impartiality he has created a series of stories both
poignant and sensitive.

Conclusion

All contemporary authors are caught in a culture that distrusts and often rejects the frameworks of belief upon which literature has been traditionally based. The contemporary writer has been provided with a cultural past that lacks meaning in the present, and with traditional fictional modes that he may find are no longer adequate. Updike has said, "The writer now makes his mark on paper blanker than it has ever been. Our common store of assumptions has dwindled, and with it the stock of viable artistic conventions." [1]

This inability to rely on generally accepted institutions that would provide both a thematic base and a technical tradition has resulted in the contemporary author's exclusive reliance on self, which, thus isolated, may also disappear. This dependence on the individual personality to supplant the institutions lacking in our time has produced a literature as varied as the individuals who create it. Marcus Klein has written:

In the years since the end of World War II the novel in America has been: nihilistic, existential, apocalyptic, psychological; it has asserted the romantic self; it has recorded the loss of the self; it has explored the possibilities of social accommodation; it has withdrawn from social considerations; it has been radical and conservative. In form it has been loosely picaresque, it has returned to its beginnings in myth, it has been contrived with a cunningness of technique

virtually decadent, it has been purely self-reflexive and re-
spondent to its own development. And the novel has died.[2]

At least one novel by Updike could be fitted into
almost any of these technical and thematic categories.
Rabbit, Run and *The Centaur* have been categorized as
existentialist novels; [3] Skeeter is apocalyptic in *Rabbit
Redux;* at least one critic has treated *Of the Farm* in
exclusively psychological terms.[4] Although Updike's duality seems to preclude the annihilation of self, with the
loss of spirit Rabbit becomes, by his own admission,
"nobody" at the end of each of his novels. Returning to
Klein's list, we. can see how various novels have "explored the possibilities of social accommodation," while
the younger Rabbit was at least tempted to "withdraw
from social considerations." *Rabbit Redux* and *Couples*
could be categorized as "both radical and conservative."

Updike is similarly variable in the formal rather than
thematic classifications that Klein makes. There is of
course the return to myth in *The Centaur.* I suppose that
in *Couples,* Piet's travels, from bed to bed, might be
viewed as a version of the picaresque. Although we would
deny that it is "virtually decadent," there has certainly
been what even sympathetic critics would call a "cunningness of technique" in Updike's novels.

This summary may go to show the ultimate inap-
plicability of such categories (which is, of course, Klein's
whole intention), as it simultaneously demonstrates the
scope of Updike's fiction. Certainly Updike misses the
ideal past, a time when the writer could depend upon a
"common store of assumptions," when the paper he wrote
on was far from blank. Updike idealizes this past as a
time when man was wholly integrated, when the spiritual
and carnal were not mutually exclusive, when the natural
world was linked by mythical meaning to the supernatural.

Updike's nostalgia for such a past is a constant theme

in his fiction. We see it at first, strongly presented, by
the older people in the earlier novels—Hook in *The Poorhouse Fair*, the grandfather in *The Centaur*. In *Couples*,
however, the older generation has disappeared; Piet's
parents are dead, as is the past they represent. It remains
for him only to recognize and accept this fact. With the
burning of the church in *Couples* the failure of contemporary Christianity is symbolically recognized, and
Updike moves to the entirely secular world of *Rabbit
Redux*. Yet in *A Month of Sundays* Updike attempts to
recapture a pre-Puritan past; one critic has called Marshfield a "Chaucerian figure if ever there was one—praising
the Lord with his trousers down." [5] In *Marry Me* the
protagonist's futile expectation of "an act of God"
marks him as anachronistic, and in *The Coup*, Ellellou's
Islamic devotion leads to drought in a nation that in its
lack of modernization is a rare relic of the past.

Since Updike's concern often deals with the relation
between the physical and spiritual experience, his use of
metaphor reflects this concern and conveys it to the
reader. Metaphorical language is, after all, an assertion
that a reality exists beyond the literal. With the use of
metaphor, all writers affirm that physical experience has
a connection with mental or spiritual experience. As the
distinction between mental or spiritual experience implies,
I am dealing with two different areas here, the literary
and the theological. For most contemporary writers, the
use of metaphor remains literary rather than theological;
their use of metaphorical language does not imply what
we would call a theological parallel. But Updike's use of
metaphor often reflects a religious analogue, reinforcing
his view of "the world as layered, and as there being
something up there." [6]

Thus for Updike the literary experience imitates the
wished-for theological experience, in which the image exists as an incarnation of the author's intention. In other
words, by his repeated use of metaphorical language,

Updike is voicing the hope that the connection between the physical and spiritual worlds can be made. Thus the author becomes a creator; Updike has said, "Indeed, in combinative richness the written word rivals, almost blasphemously, Creation itself." [7]

The world that Updike, in the past twenty-two years, has created for us from the written word is richly varied indeed. It is unreasonable to expect an artist to produce works that show steady progress; it is impossible to judge "progress" without the test of time in any case. While we can, perhaps, expect improvement in each subsequent model of a manufacturer's product, an author's literary output is a different matter. When a writer is as generous with his work as Updike, he leaves himself open to a kind of criticism that less prolific writers avoid. We, unfairly, expect improvement; we expect variation; and we suspect, unjustly, that quantity affects quality.

I would argue that we get both quality and variation in Updike's novels and short stories. When I am asked which is the best of Updike's novels, I must answer with five or six titles: *Rabbit, Run, The Centaur, Rabbit Redux, A Month of Sundays, The Coup*—each of these seems to me exceptional, but each in a different way. Other critics choose other titles. And Updike has, we hope, at least twenty or twenty-five more years of writing still ahead of him. If his past productiveness continues, this may well mean that we have twenty or twenty-five more books to look forward to.

Notes

Introduction

1. John Updike, *Picked-Up Pieces*, p. 519.
2. Ibid.
3. Jane Howard, "Can a Nice Novelist Finish First?" p. 80.
4. See reviews of Tillich by Updike reprinted in *Assorted Prose*, pp. 282–283, and *Picked-Up Pieces*, pp. 123–124.
5. Updike, *Assorted Prose*, pp. 273–282, and *Picked-Up Pieces*, pp. 88–90, 125–126.
6. Howard, "Can a Nice Novelist," p. 80.
7. Ibid., p. 76.

1. *The Poorhouse Fair*

1. See Joyce Markle, *Fighters and Lovers*, pp. 27–28, for a fuller discussion of the quilt.
2. Jane Howard, "Can a Nice Novelist Finish First?" p. 81. Also Updike, *Picked-Up Pieces*, p. 503.

2. *Rabbit, Run*

1. The most successful discussion of the quest motif is Joseph Waldmeir's "It's the Going That's Important, Not the Getting There," pp. 13–27.
2. Robert Detweiler, *John Updike*, p. 6. David Galloway, on the other hand, describes Rabbit as an "absurd hero." David Galloway, *The Absurd Hero in American Fiction*, p. 21.
3. Joyce Markle, *Fighters and Lovers*, p. 43.

3. *The Centaur*

1. For a fuller discussion of the novel as mock epic see Suzanne Henning Uphaus, *"The Centaur,"* pp. 24–36.
2. Updike, *Picked-Up Pieces,* p. 503.
3. Joyce Markle was the first critic to notice the relationship between the volvox and Caldwell's role; see *Fighters and Lovers,* p. 72.
4. Updike, *Picked-Up Pieces,* p. 499.
5. Jane Howard, "Can a Nice Novelist Finish First?" p. 80.

4. *Of the Farm*

1. Updike, *Picked-Up Pieces,* p. 83.
2. Ibid., p. 502.
3. Ibid., p. 83.

5. *Couples*

1. Updike, *Picked-Up Pieces,* p. 505.
2. "View From the Catacombs," *Time,* 26 April 1968, p. 66.
3. Updike, *Picked-Up Pieces,* p. 503.
4. Ibid., p. 504.
5. Ibid.
6. Updike, *Assorted Prose,* p. 284.
7. See Robert Detweiler's book *John Updike,* pp. 138–142, for the best discussion of de Rougemont's influence in *Couples.*
8. Updike, *Assorted Prose,* p. 299.
9. Charles T. Samuels, *John Updike,* p. 36.
10. For a variety of such readings see Paula and Nick Backscheider, "Updike's *Couples,*" p. 48; Rachael Burchard, *John Updike: Yea Sayings,* pp. 128–129; Joyce Markle, *Fighters and Lovers,* p. 125; Robert Detweiler, *John Updike,* p. 137.

6. *Bech: A Book*

1. The quotations in this paragraph are from Updike, *Picked-Up Pieces*, pp. 505–506.
2. Ibid., p. 17.
3. Ibid., p. 507.
4. Ibid., p. 508.

7. *Rabbit Redux*

1. Wayne Falke, *"Rabbit Redux,"* p. 62.
2. Robert Alter, "Updike, Malamud, and the Fire This Time," p. 73.

8. *A Month of Sundays*

1. For a fuller discussion of some of the views presented here see Suzanne Henning Uphaus, "The Unified Vision of *A Month of Sundays*," pp. 5–16.

11. SOME SHORT STORIES

1. Robert Detweiler, *John Updike*, p. 65.
2. Ibid., p. 68.
3. A few of the Maples stories appear in each of Updike's collections of short stories with the exception of *Olinger Stories*. "Separating" and "Here Come the Maples," the last two in *Too Far To Go*, also appear in *Problems and Other Stories*, a collection largely concerned with the adjustments of divorce and re-marriage to be made by parents and children.
4. Erica Jong, *"Too Far To Go* by John Updike," p. 37.
5. Ibid.

Conclusion

1. Updike, *Picked-Up Pieces*, p. 17.
2. Marcus Klein, ed., *The American Novel Since World War II* (New York: Fawcett Premier Books, 1969), p. 18.
3. See, for instance, Sidney Finkelstein's chapter on Updike in *Existentialism and Alienation in American Literature*, pp. 243–252. Also see Joyce Markle, *Fighters and Lovers*, pp. 55–60.
4. Markle's chapter on *Of the Farm* is entitled "Psychological Considerations," *Fighters and Lovers*, pp. 84–105.
5. Erica Jong, *"Too Far To Go,"* p. 36.
6. Updike, *Picked-Up Pieces*, p. 502.
7. John Updike, "The Written Word," *Wilson Quarterly* 3 (1977): p. 154.

Bibliography

1. WORKS BY JOHN UPDIKE

The Carpentered Hen and Other Tame Creatures. New York: Harper & Brothers, 1958.

The Poorhouse Fair. New York: Alfred A. Knopf, 1959.

The Same Door. New York: Alfred A. Knopf, 1959.

Rabbit, Run. New York: Alfred A. Knopf, 1960.

Pigeon Feathers and Other Stories. New York: Alfred A. Knopf, 1962.

The Centaur. New York: Alfred A. Knopf, 1963.

Telephone Poles and Other Poems. New York: Alfred A. Knopf, 1963.

Olinger Stories. New York: Vintage Books, 1964.

Of the Farm. New York: Alfred A. Knopf, 1965.

Assorted Prose. New York: Alfred A. Knopf, 1965.

The Music School. New York: Alfred A. Knopf, 1966.

Couples. New York: Alfred A. Knopf, 1968.

Midpoint and Other Poems. New York: Alfred A. Knopf, 1969.

Bech: A Book. New York: Alfred A. Knopf, 1970.

Rabbit Redux. New York: Alfred A. Knopf, 1971.

Museums and Women and Other Stories. New York: Alfred A. Knopf, 1972.

Buchanan Dying. New York: Alfred A. Knopf, 1974.

Picked-Up Pieces. New York: Alfred A. Knopf, 1975.

A Month of Sundays. New York: Alfred A. Knopf, 1975.

Marry Me. New York: Alfred A. Knopf, 1976.

Tossing and Turning: Poems. New York: Alfred A. Knopf, 1977.

The Coup. New York: Alfred A. Knopf, 1978.

Too Far To Go: The Maples Stories. New York: Fawcett Crest Books, 1979.

Problems. New York: Alfred A. Knopf, 1979.

2. WORKS ABOUT JOHN UPDIKE AND INTERVIEWS

Adler, Renata. "Arcadia, Pa." *The New Yorker,* 13 April 1963, pp. 182–188.

Aldridge, John. "An Askew Halo for John Updike." *Saturday Review,* 27 June 1970, pp. 25–27, 35.

———. "The Private Vice of John Updike." In *Time to Murder and Create: The Contemporary Novel in Crisis,* pp. 164–170. New York: David McKay Co., 1964.

Alter, Robert. "Updike, Malamud, and the Fire This Time." *Commentary,* October 1972, pp. 68–74.

Backsheider, Paula and Nick. "Updike's *Couples*: Squeak in the Night." *Modern Fiction Studies* 20 (1974) : 45–52.

Brenner, Gerry. "*Rabbit, Run:* John Updike's Criticism of the 'Return to Nature.' " *Twentieth Century Literature* 12 (1966), pp. 3–14.

Burchard, Rachael C. *John Updike: Yea Sayings.* Carbondale: Southern Illinois University Press, 1971.

Burgess, Anthony. "Language, Myth, and Mr. Updike." *Commonweal,* 11 February 1966, pp. 557–559.

Burhans, Clinton S., Jr. "Things Falling Apart: Structure and Theme in *Rabbit, Run." Studies in the Novel* 5 (1973) : 336–351.

Detweiler, Robert. *John Updike.* New York: Twayne, 1972.

———. "John Updike and the Indictment of Culture-Protestantism." In *Four Spiritual Crises in Mid-Century American Fiction,* pp. 14–24. Gainesville: University of Florida Press, 1964.

———. "Updike's *Couples*: Eros Demythologized." *Twentieth Century Literature* 17 (1971), pp. 235–246.

Ditsky, John. "Roth, Updike, and the High Expense of Spirit." *University of Windsor Review,* Fall 1969, pp. 111–120.

Doner, Dean. "Rabbit Angstrom's Unseen World." *New World Writing* 20 (1962) : 58–75.

Falke, Wayne. "*Rabbit Redux:* Time/Order/God." *Modern Fiction Studies,* Spring 1974, pp. 59–75.

Finkelstein, Sidney. "Acceptance of Alienation: John Updike and James Purdy." In *Existentialism and Alienation in*

American Literature, pp. 243–252. New York: International Publishers, 1965.

Gado, Frank. "A Conversation with John Updike." *The Idol*, Spring 1971, pp. 3–32. Reprinted in *First Person*, pp. 80–109. Syracuse, N.Y.: Syracuse University Press, 1973.

Galloway, David D. "The Absurd Man as Saint: The Novels of John Updike." *Modern Fiction Studies*, Summer 1964, pp. 111–127. Reprinted in *The Absurd Hero in American Fiction: Updike, Styron, Bellow, Salinger*, pp. 21–50. Austin: University of Texas Press, 1966 (Rev. Ed., 1970).

Gingher, Robert S. "Has Updike Anything to Say?" *Modern Fiction Studies*, Spring 1974, pp. 97–105.

Hamilton, Alice and Kenneth. *The Elements of John Updike*. Grand Rapids, Mich.: William B. Eerdmans, 1970.

Harper, Howard M., Jr. "John Updike: The Intrinsic Problem of Human Existence." In his *Desperate Faith: A Study of Bellow, Salinger, Mailer, Baldwin, and Updike*, pp. 162–190. Chapel Hill: University of North Carolina Press, 1967.

Hendin, Josephine. *Vulnerable People*, pp. 88–99. New York: Oxford University Press, 1978.

Hicks, Granville. "Generations of the Fifties: Malamud, Gold, and Updike." In Nona Balakian and Charles Simmons, eds. *The Creative Present: Notes on Contemporary American Fiction*, pp. 213–237. New York: Doubleday, 1963.

———. "John Updike." In *Literary Horizons*, pp. 107–133. New York: New York University Press, 1970.

Howard, Jane. "Can a Nice Novelist Finish First?" *Life*, 4 November 1966, pp. 74–82.

Hunt, George, S. J. "Updike's Omega-Shaped Shelter: Structure and Psyche in *A Month of Sundays*." *Critique*, Spring 1978, pp. 48–64.

———. "Updike's Pilgrims in a World of Nothingness." *Thought*, December 1978, pp. 384–400.

Jong, Erica. "*Too Far to Go* by John Updike." *New Republic*, September 1979, pp. 36–37.

Lodge, David. "Post-Pill Paradise Lost: John Updike's *Couples*." In his *The Novelist at the Crossroads and*

Other Essays on Fiction and Criticism, pp. 237–244. Ithaca, N.Y.: Cornell University Press, 1972.

Mailer, Norman. "Norman Mailer vs. Nine Writers." *Esquire*, July 1963, pp. 63–69, 105.

Markle, Joyce B. *Fighters and Lovers: Theme in the Novels of John Updike*. New York: New York University Press, 1973.

Myers, David. "The Questing Fear: Christian Allegory in John Updike's *The Centaur*." *Twentieth Century Literature* 17 (1971): 73–82.

Novak, Michael. "Updike's Quest for Liturgy." *Commonwealth*, 10 May 1963, pp. 192–195.

Oates, Joyce Carol. "Updike's American Comedies." *Modern Fiction Studies*, Autumn 1975, pp. 459–472.

O'Connor, William Van. "John Updike and William Styron: The Burden of Talent." In Harry T. Moore, ed. *Contemporary American Novelists*, pp. 205–221. Carbondale: Southern Illinois University Press, 1964.

Podhoretz. Norman. "A Dissent on Updike." *Show*, April 1963, pp. 49–52. Reprinted in *Doings and Undoings: The Fifties and After in American Writing*, pp. 251–257. New York: Farrar, Straus & Giroux, 1964.

Regan, Robert Alton. "Updike's Symbol of the Center." *Modern Fiction Studies*, Spring 1974, pp. 77–96.

Rhode, Eric. "BBC Interview with John Updike." *The Listener*, 81 (1969): 862–864.

———. "Grabbing Dilemmas: John Updike Talks about God, Love and the American Identity." *Vogue*, 1 February 1971, pp. 140–141, 184–185.

Samuels, Charles Thomas. "The Art of Fiction XLIII: John Updike." *Paris Review*, Winter 1968, pp. 84–117.

———. *John Updike*. Minneapolis: University of Minnesota Press, 1969.

———. "Updike on the Present." *New Republic*, 20 November 1971, pp. 29–30.

Schopen, Bernard A. "Faith, Morality, and the Novels of John Updike." *Twentieth Century Literature* 24 (1978), pp. 523–535.

Siegel, Gary. "Rabbit Runs Down." In Peary, Gerald, and Roger Shatzkin, eds. *The Modern American Novel and the Movies.* New York: Frederick Ungar Publishing Co., 1978.

Sheed, Wilfred. "Play in Tarbox." *New York Times Book Review,* 7 April 1968, pp. 1, 30–33. Reprinted in *The Morning After: Selected Essays and Reviews,* pp. 36–42. New York: Farrar, Straus & Giroux, 1971.

Stafford, William T. " 'The Curious Greased Grace' of John Updike: Some of His Critics and the American Tradition." *Journal of Modern Literature,* 2 (1972) : 569–575.

———. "Updike FourFiveSix, "Just Like That": An Essay Review." *Modern Fiction Studies,* Spring 1974, pp. 115–120.

Strandberg, Victor. "John Updike and the Changing of the Gods." *Mosaic* 12: 157–175.

Stubbs, J. C. "Search for Perfection in *Rabbit, Run.*" *Critique: Studies in Modern Fiction* 10 (1968) : 94–101.

Tanner, Tony. "A Compromised Environment." In *City of Words: American Fiction, 1950–1970,* pp. 273–294. New York: Harper & Row, 1971.

Taylor, Larry E. *Pastoral and Anti-Pastoral Patterns in John Updike's Fiction.* Carbondale: Southern Illinois University Press, 1971.

Uphaus, Suzanne Henning. *"The Centaur:* Updike's Mock Epic." *Journal of Narrative Technique,* Winter 1977, pp. 24–36.

———. "The Unified Vision of *A Month of Sundays.*" *University of Windsor Review,* Spring-Summer 1977, pp. 5–16.

Vargo, Edward P. "The Necessity of Myth in Updike's *The Centaur.*" *PMLA,* 85 (1973) : 452–460.

———. *Rainstorms and Fire: Ritual in the Novels of John Updike.* Port Washington, N.Y.: Kennikat Press, 1973.

Vickery, John. *"The Centaur:* Myth, History, and Narrative." *Modern Fiction Studies,* Spring 1974, pp. 29–43.

Waldmeier, Joseph. "It's the Going That's Important, Not the Getting There: Rabbit's Questing Non-Quest." *Modern Fiction Studies,* Spring 1974, pp. 13–27.

Ward, John A. "John Updike's Fiction." *Critique: Studies in Modern Fiction,* Spring-Summer 1962, pp. 27–40.

3. BIBLIOGRAPHIES OF JOHN UPDIKE

Meyer, Arlin, and Olivas, Michael. "Criticism of John Updike: A Selected Checklist." *Modern Fiction Studies*,
Spring 1974, pp. 121–133.

Olivas, Michael. *An Annotated Bibliography of John Updike Criticism, 1967–1973, and a Checklist of His Works*.
New York: Garland Press, 1975.

Sokoloff, B. A., and Arnason, David E. *John Updike: A
Comprehensive Bibliography*. Darby, Pa.: Darby Press,
1970. Folcroft, Pa.: Folcroft Press, 1971. Norwood, Pa.:
Norwood Press, 1973.

Taylor, C. Clarke. *John Updike: A Bibliography*. Kent, Ohio:
Kent State University Press, 1968.

Index

MODERN LITERATURE MONOGRAPHS

In the same series (continued from page ii)